Civil Rights Journey

The Story of a White Southerner Coming of Age during the Civil Rights Revolution

To Adam McGraw

with best wishes from c sj

for of your parents

Joseph Howell

authorHOUSE®

To the Holt family—
Jack and Dovanna (in memoriam),
Noah (Jackie), and Nathaniel

AuthorHouse™
1663 Liberty Drive
Bloomington, IN 47403
www.authorhouse.com
Phone: 1-800-839-8640

First published by AuthorHouse 04/27/2011

ISBN: 978-1-4567-6208-7 (sc)
ISBN: 978-1-4567-6209-4 (e)
ISBN: 978-1-4567-6207-0 (dj)
Library of Congress Control Number: 2011906165

Printed in the United States of America

This book is printed on acid-free paper.

*The views expressed in this work are solely those of the author and do not necessarily reflect
the views of the publisher, and the publisher hereby disclaims any responsibility for them.*

Contents

Appreciation vii

Foreword ix

Introduction xi

**Part I: Growing Up White in the South during the Last
Decades of Jim Crow, 1942–1966**   **1**

Chapter One: What's Wrong with This Picture? 3

Chapter Two: Polio Kid...9

Chapter Three: Separate and Unequal 20

Chapter Four: Down but Not Out..25

Chapter Five: Change Begins 34

Chapter Six: College Years...40

Chapter Seven: The Movement Picks Up Steam 48

Chapter Eight: Marching in Charlotte....................................57

Chapter Nine: Off to New York City..73

Part II: Civil Rights Diary *with Embry Howell*   **87**

Diary of Joe Howell: Summer 1966..89

Part III: Aftermath, 1966–1968   **157**

Chapter Ten: Back to New York 159

Chapter Eleven: The Southwest Georgia Project 167

Chapter Twelve: 1968..171

Postscript...177

Suggested Reading 185

Appreciation

This book would never have been written without Embry Howell. She is the one who discovered the diary in our attic, read it first, typed it all up, provided the annotations, assisted with the final editing, and encouraged me to publish it. She was also a major participant in the drama; and without her encouragement, it is doubtful that we would have made the trip to southwest Georgia in the first place. I am deeply indebted to her in so many ways, and this is just as much her book as it is mine.

Just as it takes a village to raise a child, it takes a lot of friends to get a book out. Two in particular stand out—Tony Abbott, an outstanding English professor at Davidson College, and Hank Ackerman, a former Associated Press editor and bureau chief. Their comments and edits came in the book's early stages; for their effort and sharp eyes, I am grateful. But there were a lot more. Bill Ferris, a good college friend, now a noted scholar of Southern history and culture, gave me encouragement and advice. Also invaluable were Union Seminary friends who worked with us in southwest Georgia in 1966, Ashley Wiltshire and Ed Feaver. Among other things they gave me assurance that my diary of the southwest Georgia civil rights experience was not too far off base. Ashley's wife, Susan, was very helpful as well in providing editing suggestions. There were other friends and family who gave helpful advice, including Bob Bremner, Buck Cole, Bill Marks, Mike Martin, and our supportive children and their spouses. Last but not least, for any book to get to press you need a good editor; and no one is better than my nephew, Alex Martin, who served as copyeditor. For everyone's help and encouragement, thanks.

Finally, I am profoundly grateful and moved by the words of Janet Hampton in the foreword to this book. Just before sending the manuscript off to the printer, I provided a copy to Jan, now retired from a distinguished career as professor at George Washington University and a friend from my days serving on the Humanities Council of Washington, D.C. (of which she was chair). Much to my surprise she got back to me in a matter of days with her "reflections." Those comments now set the stage for the story you are about to read.

The diary—and the book—would not have been the same without the Holt family: Dovanna and Jack and their sons, Noah (Jackie) and Nathaniel. They took us under their wing and made us a part of their family at a time when it was extremely dangerous for blacks in the South to take in white "outside agitators." We were touched by their love, good humor, and courage. That is why the book is dedicated to them.

Foreword

As I was reading *Civil Rights Journey* I found myself becoming totally captivated by the story that it conveyed. So many aspects of it resonated with me and brought forth feelings and emotions that I experienced during the years that it portrays. The depth and complexity of Joe Howell's Nashville, revealed from the perspective of his life within his family and community, fleshed out the essence that was absent from my personal experience in that city as a student (when I was sixteen to eighteen years old) at Fisk University. It introduced me to a community that I never had the opportunity to know. With the exception of a few exchange students from Oberlin and a few international students at Fisk, my social contact with the white world was limited to a few Fisk professors and a handful of Vanderbilt students who were members of the Newman Club. On reflection it amazes me just how totally and methodically institutionalized segregation was at that time. The separation of races (and classes) could not have been more precise and decisive (and impassive?) if the scalpel of a skilled surgeon had brought it about.

Civil Rights Journey is an account of a young man's coming of age, a young man shaped early in life by the crucibles of polio and segregation (both by decree and by custom) and later by that of the civil rights movement. Joe Howell's story depicts the effects of human vulnerability and of human cruelty. The lingering effects of polio made him at times the object of bullying and derision, perhaps thus increasing his sensitivity to such cruelties manifested in the system of segregation. The reader shares the hopes, doubts, and at times despair that form Joe as he tries to wrest meaning from his experiences and determine what his path in life should be. Along his path Joe encounters and tries to reconcile the complexities and contradictions of the philosophies of members of SNCC and the Black Panthers, as well as those of his seminary colleagues and other volunteers who participated in that civil rights summer. The structure of this memoir is enhanced by the voice of Embry Howell, Joe's wife. It complements Joe's well. The thread of her voice is woven into the fabric of Joe's story in the account of the civil rights summer that they shared, adding a richness of texture to that account. The story of the Holt family, also, is a compelling part of the memoir. It enriches the narrative. The Holts were a black family who embraced the Howells and added to their understanding of the reality not only of segregation in their community of Albany, Georgia, but also of injustices across our nation. Their story is a vivid portrait of the complexity of the black experience. The reader comes to know and care about the Holts and is inspired by the outcome of their story.

Civil Rights Journey offers the reader a multilayered account of a young man born in the pre–civil rights South, sheltered by a code of customs that privileged the white middle class at the expense of blacks and poor whites, and of his formation and moral development shaped by the crucible of his civil rights journey.

—Janet Hampton
January 2011

Introduction

In early 2002 while cleaning our dusty attic in our home in Washington, D.C., my wife, Embry, suddenly turned to me holding an old black notebook. "You will never believe what I found," she exclaimed, smiling. "This is the diary you kept when we were working in the civil rights movement in southwest Georgia in 1966."

"Come on," I replied. "I didn't write a journal when we were down there."

"Yes you did, and here it is."

I started thumbing through the worn pages, and the experience all started coming back.

Neither of us read the whole diary, thinking we would get back to it later. Instead we promptly forgot about it for several years, until Embry went to spend a summer in Tanzania evaluating a health care initiative. Since she was going to have a lot of time alone, she took the diary with her. In a labor of love, she typed up the whole thing, along with her own comments. When she got back I read it all, most of it for the first time. I could not believe what we lived through that summer—the excitement, fear, frustration, and hope, and probably most of all the ambivalence as to what we were doing there and what we were accomplishing. We both thought the diary had merit because we did not think there were many firsthand experiences written by white people about what it was like at ground level working with the Student Nonviolent Coordinating Committee, known as SNCC (pronounced "Snick"), in the Deep South in the 1960s. The diary was both an account of one young couple's experience in the civil rights movement and a coming of age story, at times naive and "politically incorrect" but honest and genuine.

The initial response by several readers was that the diary needed some history and more personal information wrapped around it to give it perspective. I did what they suggested, and the result is what you are about to read. I have tried to bring in pertinent information about my growing up in Nashville as it related to my civil rights journey and to show what was happening in the civil rights movement at each stage in my own life. The result is part memoir, part diary, and part history. The history part is not intended to be definitive in any sense. I have tried to provide enough information about my own life and about the civil rights movement for the reader to put our civil rights journey into context.

★★★

When I was born in Nashville, Tennessee, the South was totally segregated, and Jim Crow laws governed the way things worked. Blacks rode in the back of the bus. Lunch counters and restrooms were segregated by race. Blacks and whites attended different schools, played in different professional sports leagues, and there were virtually no black elected public officials. Income disparities were enormous, and the main jobs available for African Americans were the kinds of jobs white people did not want to do—cleaning homes and businesses, picking up garbage, cutting grass, and generally serving white folks. "Literacy tests" and other obstacles kept most black people off the registered voting lists. This is well-known history, and most people now acknowledge that the Jim Crow system was wrong. Thankfully it did not stay this way for a whole lot longer, as many whites hoped it would in the 1950s. That things did change in my lifetime in such profound ways is still hard to comprehend fully. In the early 1950s who would have predicted that in the 1960s segregation as we knew it would start to disappear and that in the early twenty-first century we would have elected an African American president?

This book is about being part of that history. I was born in 1942 and lived in the South until after I graduated from college. In hindsight, it is obvious that the first hints of change came to Nashville when I was very young. The Supreme Court decided *Brown v. Board of Education* in 1954. The Montgomery, Alabama, bus boycott that initiated the civil rights movement occurred in 1956. The first sit-ins—at a Woolworth's lunch counter in Greensboro, North Carolina—took place in February 1960 when I was a senior in high school. Similar sit-ins in downtown Nashville followed that month. In fact Nashville was one of the key cities where civil rights strategy was being mapped out. As a teenager living in an all-white, upper-income neighborhood, however, I was only vaguely aware of these happenings.

There is a lot in part 1 of this book about my experience with polio, which I contracted in 1952, coincidently the year that *Brown v. Board of Education* was first filed in federal courts. I bring in this experience because I believe it enabled me to identify with others who were struggling or suffering in one way or another. Were it not for polio, I doubt I would have followed the journey that I did on civil rights.

By my freshmen year at Davidson College in North Carolina, protests against segregation were beginning to happen throughout the South, and it was hard not to realize that something big was going on. During my senior year, along with a handful of my fellow students, I organized and led a march in Charlotte supporting the legislation that would become the Civil Rights Act of 1964. Harmless as the event might seem now, it created quite a stir in Charlotte and in Davidson and immediately thrust me into the limelight.

Following my graduation from Davidson I moved to New York City to attend Union Theological Seminary, a nondenominational Protestant seminary with a reputation for progressive theology and social action. One of my classmates at Union was Charles Sherrod, an African American who was one of the early leaders of SNCC, the most radical civil rights group at the time. He recruited me and about a dozen other Union students to work with him in the "movement" in southwest Georgia in 1966. I had just married Embry Martin, also a Southerner, in December 1965. Along with fellow Union Seminary students, we followed Charlie to Albany and then to Baker County, a remote and beautiful area in Georgia's far southwestern tip. While we were there, I kept the diary that was long forgotten until it turned up in a pile of scrapbooks in our attic forty years later.

The story that follows is about how we got involved in the civil rights movement and what that experience was like, but it is about a lot more as well. It is about my struggle to overcome the adversity of polio, my search for meaning and values, and how religion influenced my search. It is about growing up.

PART I

Growing Up White in the South during the Last Decades of Jim Crow, 1942–1966

Chapter One:

What's Wrong with This Picture?

You might say I peaked early. At age five I was the King of the Mardi Gras. The event took place at a prestigious hotel in downtown Nashville. I put on a king's crown of red velvet and white pearls, wore a white, laced outfit, and paraded down the center aisle of a large auditorium, packed with anxious onlookers, holding the hand of my queen, Patsy Gardner, also age five. My mother was nervous and preoccupied with getting my costume just right. Someone helped her put makeup and lipstick on me, much to my embarrassment. Other children our age were dressed as court attendants, guards, and ladies-in-waiting. It was dark going down the aisle. There were spotlights shining in our faces and lots of flashes from cameras held by professional photographers. The next day my photo appeared in the society pages of the *Nashville Banner*, the town's conservative newspaper.

I had arrived. I was part of Nashville society.

I have no idea what the Mardi Gras was all about or why I was the king, but it tells you a lot about the Nashville I grew up in. People in the part of town where my family lived—Belle Meade—seemed to enjoy privilege and entitlement. Some of the homes were mansions. Country clubs were important, as were various charity events sponsored by the Junior League and other well-intentioned organizations. I presume the Mardi Gras festival that I presided over was a fundraiser for some worthy cause. Everyone I knew lived in a big house, and practically everyone I knew had a black maid who prepared meals of fresh biscuits, fried chicken, and collard greens and cleaned the house. Husbands went to work every day in downtown Nashville, and wives stayed home to oversee the property and be sure the children got the proper upbringing. Birthday parties for children were often elaborate. There was a distinction between old money and new money. People with new money often lived in the big mansions, but the old money was the good money. My father was a banker, as was my grandfather. In those days bankers did not make the kinds of salaries they do today, so while we lived comfortably, we lived fairly modestly—in an average house in a nice neighborhood, no fancy cars and no extravagant vacations. But the money we did have seemed to be mainly old money, and that was good. There were four of us—my father, mother, me, and my little brother, five years younger than me.

It is true that Nashville was already home to the Grand Ole Opry, but few people of my parents' generation had ever attended the Opry, and many would rather not be seen rubbing shoulders with "rednecks," as country music fans were often called. That all changed years later as country music became one of the engines of the Nashville economy; but in those days, living in Belle Meade you were only vaguely aware of its existence. Nashville was not Music City. Nashville was "the Athens of the South," with excellent universities such as Vanderbilt and Fisk and six or seven others and with the only full-size replica of the Parthenon in the world. It was a city of culture and enlightenment, horses and steeplechases, cocktail parties on verandas overlooking luxuriant gardens with black waiters in white jackets serving scotch and sodas on silver trays. It was debutante parties, golf at country clubs, high school football games on Friday nights, and church on Sunday. It was green hills and sparkling rivers only minutes away from fine neighborhoods. It was, I thought then and still think now, one of the most beautiful places on earth.

I did not understand what being part of Nashville society meant at the time, but what I did clearly understand at age five was that my being King of the Mardi Gras was something special. Maybe I was entitled. After all, my grandfather had been the president of a Nashville bank, and my father was an up-and-coming banker (and eventually became a bank president himself). My parents were pillars of the community. They both belonged to various social organizations and were active in Christ Episcopal Church downtown, which was known for producing bishops. My father was the adult leader of my Cub Scout troop, senior warden of the church (the highest position for a layperson), and president of the country club. He coached neighborhood baseball and took me fly fishing as soon as I was old enough to hold a rod. My mother was head of the Women of the Episcopal Church, not just of Nashville but of the whole state. And she was always there when I needed her. I also had several neighborhood friends and was part of what we called a neighborhood gang. Life was good.

So what was wrong with this picture?

Well, at that time in my life, not very much, though there were some unanswered questions and hints that all was not perfect.

★★★

My best friend in Nashville about the time I was King of the Mardi Gras was Frederick. Frederick was almost exactly my age, and my mother would arrange for him to come to my grandmother's house, where we played together regularly. He was lots of fun to be with, had lots of energy, and loved to climb trees and play behind my grandmother's spooky garage. We played cowboys and Indians, hide and seek, and a number of make-believe games. Frederick's father, Alfred, worked at the train yard in the heart of downtown Nashville, and occasionally he would allow Frederick and me to meet him there where he would hoist us up into the cab of a giant locomotive and let us pretend we were driving it.

Then one day, not long after my Mardi Gras debut, my mother told me that Frederick would not be playing with me anymore. I could not believe it. He was my best friend. What had I done wrong? What had he done wrong? There must be some explanation.

"Well," she said, "you didn't do anything wrong, and he didn't do anything wrong. It is just after a certain age colored boys and white boys don't play together anymore."

Frederick, colored? I thought about it for a minute and then realized that, yes, I guess he was colored. It had never really occurred to me. Frederick's father was the nephew of Emma, our cook and housekeeper. They all were colored.

When I asked my mother why colored boys and white boys couldn't play together after a certain age, she blushed and had a strained look on her face. "That is just the way it is, and someday you will understand." I never saw Frederick again.

I did not grow up in a racist household, and my guess is that there were many families in Nashville like mine. The only time I heard the

N word used in my home was when a neighborhood friend of mine said something about "those Niggers in East Nashville." My mother glared at him for a moment and then said, "Young man, you will *never* use that word in our home or in our yard again ever. *Ever.* Do you understand?"

The term "Nigra," however, was used occasionally by respectable white persons in Belle Meade and was in those days explained as the white southern pronunciation of "Negro." But in our house we didn't talk about "Nigras." African Americans were simply "colored."

To say that my parents were not racists is not to deny that they were participants in institutional racism. Almost everyone—that is, everyone white—was a participant in institutional racism in those days in the South. In the 1950s there was no choice. Even in a progressive border state like Tennessee, Jim Crow ruled the land. Jim Crow laws were the local and state laws passed after Reconstruction. They required the legal separation of whites and African Americans in just about every aspect of life—schools, lunch counters, restrooms, public transportation, movie theaters, sports events—almost everything.

Not only did practically everyone in Belle Meade—and just about everywhere else in the South, for that matter—accept this as a fact of life, it gave cover to outright acts of racism. Maybe you did not hear the N word that much in respectable Nashville households, but you surely heard it on the school playgrounds and in the streets. Even some of my friends talked about "how stupid Niggers were," "how all Niggers smelled bad," "how jigaboos were idiots," and similar language. Even at a young age I smarted at such talk. I knew it was wrong because it did not reflect my experience and because my parents would never permit it.

The colored people I knew were almost like family. I loved Emma, the plump black woman with the kind smile who prepared my lunch, looked after me when my mom was not around, and made the best biscuits in the world. And I loved her great nephew, Frederick, my best friend. My parents always spoke kindly and respectfully of Emma and her nephew, Alfred. Besides working for the railroad, Alfred was an ordained Baptist minister and did yard work and minor carpentry on the side, often helping my father with house repairs. He was a kind and gentle person, and his son took after him. We always gave gifts to Emma and to her extended family at Christmastime, and I felt there was genuine love for them. I felt she would do anything for us; and we, anything for her and her family. To talk about how bad colored people were just did not make any sense to me.

And yet I knew even at a young age that the relationship between blacks and whites was far from being on a level playing field. Emma worked for us and did what we asked her to do. She was a servant. We called the shots. Compared to where she lived, our house was a mansion. We lived in a beautiful neighborhood. She lived in East Nashville in public housing with trash in the yards and graffiti on the walls.

But what could you do? This is just the way the world is, I told myself. Like everyone else I went along with the program. Maybe my mother was right. Someday I would understand.

There was another experience which haunts me to this day.

My mother was active in a number of civic and charitable causes that involved fundraising. In early March, a few weeks before my tenth birthday, she asked me if I would like to go with her as she canvassed people to raise money for an orphanage in Nashville. It was a Sunday morning, and we set off together just after sunrise. It was colder than usual for that time of the year. Light frost was on the ground, and a haze of smoke and smog hovered just above the rooftops as we drove from our home in Belle Meade to a neighborhood near the state capitol. I had never been to that neighborhood before. It was nothing like my neighborhood. The houses were small and narrow, wood frame with gray decaying wood and no paint. They were bunched up together, one beside another with hardly any room to squeeze through between the houses. "They call them shotgun shacks," my mother said casually as we made our way to the first house, stepping carefully up two broken steps. There was trash in the small yard—trash everywhere for that matter—and some broken toys lying under an old swing on the front porch. It did not look like anyone was home except that black smoke was coming out of the small chimney. In fact smoke was pouring out of all the chimneys, which contributed to the smog and gave an eerie appearance to the entire neighborhood. Making the scene even more bizarre was the silhouette of the state capitol rising within a stone's throw of the backyards of these homes. For all I knew we could have been on another planet.

"We are going to knock on this door?" I asked hesitantly.

"Of course we are, we have been given a list of addresses, and these are the ones on our list."

Mother knocked and we waited, then she knocked again. No answer.

Just as I was about to suggest that it was time to move on, the door opened very cautiously, leaving a space of no more than three or four inches, a space large enough to see two eyes on the face of a black woman peering out. The eyes showed fear. I wanted to crawl into a hole.

A quivering voice said, "What do you want? What do you want from me?"

My mother explained that we were raising money for a worthy cause—an orphanage—and asked if she would like to contribute.

"Just a minute," she said and excused herself, leaving the door partially open, wide enough for me to peer in. The room had practically no furniture. There was an old wooden table, a couple of broken wooden chairs, and a mattress and bedspring in the corner where an infant was sleeping. One of the windows was broken, allowing the cold Sunday morning wind into the room. Were it not for an overworked, coal-burning stove in the center of the room, the place would have been freezing.

A minute or so later she was back, and in her hand was one nickel. "I am so sorry, ma'am, I would like to give more, but this is all I got." She handed the nickel to my mother, who dropped it into the bucket that I was carrying.

"Well, that is the first one," Mother said with a smile, and off we went to the next house, where essentially the same scene repeated itself. My recollection is that almost everyone we canvassed that cold March morning put something in that bucket. Most of the time it was a nickel or a dime. In a couple of instances it was only a penny or two, and from one or two houses we received a quarter. Most of the people who answered the door were black but not all. We must have visited close to fifty homes that morning, in five or six of which were white families; but their living conditions were no better than those of the black families. By noon we had finished our list and were ready to head home. We had collected less than ten dollars.

I could not ever remember being so embarrassed. What were we doing there? We should be giving money to them. How could people live in such deplorable situations? I was in such complete disbelief that I could not even bring myself to talk about the experience with my mother. I never accompanied her again on any of her charitable fundraising missions.

Chapter Two:
Polio Kid

In the spring of 1952 at age ten, I was at the top of my young game. I was doing well in school, loved athletics (especially baseball), and was popular. I loved my parents, my neighborhood, my house, and my friends. I loved cutting the grass, pitching baseball with my teenage neighbor, playing with my little brother, and going fly fishing with my dad.

That was also the year I attended my first overnight summer camp. Probably for financial reasons, my parents decided the best bet for me was the local YMCA camp rather than the fancy, private camp in the East Tennessee mountains that most of my friends attended. Most of my cabin mates were from the other part of town—naturally they were white. They pronounced words differently from the way I did and were a pretty tough crowd. They used the N word a lot. Many in my Belle Meade neighborhood would have called them rednecks. It was a good experience because it exposed me to different kinds of people and got me out of the cocoon of Belle Meade.

In terms of my health, however, it turned out to be a disaster. I got the stomach flu and could not keep a meal down. When I returned home two weeks later, I had lost eight pounds and was almost skin and bones. My parents were horrified.

One of the reasons my parents were horrified was their fear of the plague. The plague in those days was polio. It struck innocent children at random, leaving them paralyzed, some even unable to breathe without the assistance of an iron lung. No one was safe—rich or poor, black or white; and in 1952 there was not a thing anyone could do about it. It struck me about ten days after I got back from summer camp, exhausted and emaciated.

The odd thing is that it was not until well after my fever had passed that my parents told me I had polio. I developed a high fever one evening, was rushed to the hospital for painful tests on my spinal cord, and then was taken home and put to bed. I was attended by a private nurse more or less twenty-four hours a day. She was a large black woman, probably in her thirties, a no-nonsense person who really seemed to know her stuff. Most of what I remember was having cold washrags placed on my forehead and all over my body. I did not know it, but a yellow quarantine sign had been placed next to our mailbox. My fever lasted for ten days.

How does one have an experience like this and not put two and two together? When my parents finally did tell me that I had polio, I was absolutely astonished and had mixed feelings of pride—"Wow, I've come through this and am still alive, like a war hero"—and fear— "What does this mean now?" During my fever I had asked my parents several times what was wrong with me, to which they calmly replied that I had a virus. When after hearing the truth I confronted them with this bald-faced lie, they said, first, that polio *was* a virus so it was not a lie, at least not technically, and, second, they did not want to scare me. The doctors had told them that a reaction of fear and panic could make my condition worse. I forgave them.

So what did this mean going forward? For one thing it meant my life would never be the same again. It also meant in some strange way that I would set out on a different path from that followed by most of my Nashville friends, one that would lead me to the civil rights movement.

It took time to know how serious the paralysis was. I knew that something was not right since I could not lift my right arm or sit up, and my nurse was very careful to make sure I did not do anything until the doctors had signed off. In a couple of days I was placed on a stretcher and taken to Vanderbilt Hospital for tests. The doctors asked me to try to move this limb and then that limb; and finally when I had tried to move just about every appendage in my body, they sent me home. Our family doctor returned to my house several days later to deliver the news—I had a moderate to severe case of polio with severe paralysis in my stomach muscles and in my right hand and right arm, with moderate paralysis in my right leg and minor paralysis elsewhere. What got my attention was the comment from the doctor, "Son, you better start learning how to use your left hand to write because you are sure not ever going to be able to write again with your right hand." So much for the big league pitching career.

I came down with polio in June 1952. Six months later, on December 9, 1952, Thurgood Marshall argued *Brown v. Board of Education of Topeka* before the U.S. Supreme Court. Seventeen months later, on May 17, 1954, a unanimous Supreme Court would issue the opinion that would change race relations in the United States forever. Legal segregation would be history. The South would never be the same.

The connection between polio and civil rights in my case was how polio influenced my worldview. I suppose I was a sensitive kid. I already had questions as to why there was segregation in the first place. Maybe I would have turned out the same if I had not had polio, if I had been a good athlete and comfortably ensconced in Belle Meade society. But I think not. Because of polio I developed an identification with the underdog, with people who are different, who are left out, who are marginalized. I was one of those marginalized people for several years during a critical period of growing up. You do not walk in these shoes without developing empathy, almost a bond, with others in similar circumstances. At least I didn't. And to this day I am profoundly grateful for the polio experience. Like so many other polio victims, I defied the odds and came back a lot farther and faster than any of the doctors expected. I *was* like a war hero and did return home, eventually victorious and more or less intact.

But it was not easy, and it did not happen overnight.

There was another side of the polio coin, however. I also wanted more than anything else to be "normal." I did not like being stared at, I certainly did not like being pitied, and I did not like being different. So from the summer of 1952 on, one of my primary goals in life was simply to fit in, to be part of the crowd and not stand out—"to be normal." I yearned to be the ultimate conformist.

These two goals often were in conflict with each other and not always easy to reconcile. They have been with me all my life.

★★★

So what to do next? What happens after the fever diminishes and you are left alone, unable to do the most fundamental things, like walk and eat with a knife and fork? I did not have a lot of time to feel sorry for myself. Within a few weeks I was on a train headed to Warm Springs.

Warm Springs, Georgia, was about eighty miles southwest of Atlanta. The tiny community—under one thousand people—was originally famous for its warm mineral waters and was a popular spa in the nineteenth century. Learning of these springs, Franklin Roosevelt visited the area in the mid-1920s in hopes of getting help with his paralysis, a result of the polio he contracted in 1921. Roosevelt loved being in Warm Springs and believed the warm mineral water had a medicinal effect. At that time he was already a public figure; and when word got out that Franklin Roosevelt was there because of his polio, other polio victims started showing up at the small inn where he stayed. This gave impetus to the idea of making Warm Springs a haven for people who had polio, and Roosevelt created the Georgia Warm Springs Polio Foundation. In 1926 he bought the entire resort using two-thirds of his financial resources. Over the next several years he began to transform the sleepy resort into the premier rehabilitation center for polio victims in the United States and probably in the world. He remained committed and involved in Warm Springs even when he was president. He was staying at the "Little White House"—his cottage in Warm Springs—when he suffered the stroke that killed him in 1945.

To get into Warm Springs was not easy. In 1952 fifty-eight thousand cases of polio were reported in the United States—the most ever. There were long waiting lists for admission, and only the most severe cases were eligible. One of the foremost experts in treating paralysis from polio was from Nashville, a young orthopedic surgeon, Don Iler, who had made polio his specialty. He had just returned to Nashville from Warm Springs, where he was one of the top doctors. Our family doctor—my father's second cousin, whom we always referred to as "Doctor Tom"—knew Doctor Iler, as did a number of my parents' friends. I do not know what strings were pulled, but in a matter of weeks, I was on my way down there. It was one of the best things that ever happened to me.

I was in Warm Springs from July 1952 almost until Christmas. I was a short-timer, due in large part to the fact that compared to practically everyone else there, I was in good shape.

My mother accompanied me on the train to Georgia. It turned out that not only I had polio but my father and my brother had been diagnosed with it as well, though their cases were very mild. My mother was the only one in good enough health to go with me. It was an ordeal getting me on the train since I had to be carried. A smiling, towering African American wearing a red cap and black uniform hoisted me from my wheelchair into the train. During the whole trip I was confined to a sleeper car, where my mother and I watched the world go by our windows. I had not been out of Nashville very much and had only a vague idea of what the world beyond it was like. Mile after mile, I peered through the dirty windows at small town after small town, endless green fields with cotton and soybeans and corn, and long, straight, dusty roads. I do not remember ever being bored.

What I do remember is the similarity between the shantytown behind the Tennessee state capitol in Nashville and the clusters of gray, dilapidated shotgun shacks along the railroad tracks. They seemed to line the tracks whenever we went through a city or small town. There were often people on porches and kids playing in the dusty streets. Most were African Americans, though occasionally there would be a white family or two. Most wore overalls or similar farming clothes, and the children seemed to be dressed in rags. I wondered if the Nashville shantytown I visited with my mother was more the norm than Belle Meade.

We got off the train in Atlanta, where I was again lifted by one of the black porters into a wheelchair, which was waiting for me beside the train. Beside it were two muscular, blond, young white men in white medical uniforms. They assisted my mother with our bags and pushed me through the bustling station to a white ambulance, where I was placed on a stretcher and put in the back. The two attendants sat in the front seat, talking and laughing and not paying much attention to us. My mother squeezed in beside me. About halfway into the two-hour trip the driver turned to me and asked if I would like to hear the siren. Of course I said yes, and off it went as the driver stepped on the gas, and we screeched along the two-lane highway, at one point going almost ninety miles an hour. My mother was horrified. I loved every minute.

Warm Springs was a beehive of activity. Kids of all ages were everywhere—on the sprawling lawn, in the hallways, in rooms. Kids were in wheelchairs, some propelling themselves, others being pushed by men who looked just like our driver and his buddy. Kids were on stretchers and on crutches with big iron braces on their legs. Kids were in iron lungs with their heads poking out at the end. The patients being pushed on stretchers seemed to be moving very fast, like they were late for an important appointment. There were lots of smiles and laughter, lots of banter between the polio kids and their attendants. It seemed like one huge party. I could feel the excitement. The best image I can think of to describe it is the "Never Never Land" of Peter Pan. Warm Springs was someplace special.

After all the paperwork was done, my mother kissed me goodbye. I would not see her again for six months. My father came and visited once, midway through my stay. That was the way it was at Warm Springs. Parents and family were not encouraged to visit.

I was placed in a four-bed ward with three other boys. They all had been there before I arrived, and they would be there when I left. Next to me was Rabbit Brown. He was almost fourteen and was from Vicksburg, Mississippi, had big horned-rimmed glasses, a thin face, smiled a lot, and was thoughtful and low key. On the other side of the room was Dean Belknap, a twelve-year-old from Lincoln, Nebraska. Dean had lots of black hair and spoke very slowly due to the medication he was taking for epilepsy. Next to him was Jeff Purdy, also twelve, a Holden Caulfield type of kid with curly red hair from somewhere in Connecticut outside of New York City. Jeff's father was the editor of *True Magazine,* so there were always plenty of magazines around to read about hunting, fishing, and adventure. All three of these boys had a lot more physical challenges than I did. Though I was confined to a wheelchair, I could stand on my own and was told I did not need leg braces. All three of them had leg braces and could not stand by themselves. I had been told I would never be able to write with my right hand. These boys had all been told they would never be able to walk again.

We all got along well. We had a packed schedule involving physical therapy, school classes, more therapy in the mineral waters, group programs involving speakers and performances, and supposedly quiet periods for napping and resting. In the evenings there were movies on certain days in a large theater that filled up with wheelchairs and stretchers. We made time for wheelchair races down hallway corridors, which were against the rules, and for hanging out. Since two of us were from the South and two from the North, we had endless discussions regarding the Civil War and agreed that when we all got out of Warm

Springs and returned to a normal life we would meet in Vicksburg and reenact the Civil War battle there.

We also talked about the things boys that age talk about. I was the youngest; but the other guys were beginning to show an interest in girls, and Jeff was obsessed with them. Every time a new male attendant was assigned to our room, Jeff would beckon him to his bedside and whisper in his ear if he knew how we could get hold of any "rubbers." I remember the first time I saw this happen. The attendant doubled over laughing and brought several of his friends into the room. He pointed at Jeff and whispered something to his friends, giggling. The other guys slapped each other on the back and guffawed, "Now what would he do with something like that?" This did not keep Jeff from continuing his quest the entire time I was there, though I do not believe he was ever successful. Though there were plenty of girls at Warm Springs, I do not have a specific memory of a single one.

The activity that our four-bed ward was known for was the "fight to the finish." I had a brace on my right hand involving a rubber band that pulled my thumb away from my palm. I soon discovered that this made a great slingshot for paper wads. The other guys had similar devices, so we got the idea of having paper-wad fights in the evenings after curfew. We spent much of our free time during the day carefully making paper wads; and when the lights went out, the fight to the finish was on. It was the North versus the South. Rabbit and I were the Rebels and Dean and Jeff the Yankees. The morning shift of attendants would give us a hard time about the mess of paper on the floor. We were never reported as far as I know, and the fights to the finish continued for most of the time I was there.

Miracles happened at Warm Springs. Little by little I started to regain use of some of the muscles I had lost, and in just under six months the doctors said I was ready to return home. I could walk a little and was beginning to have a little use of my arm and leg. Just before Christmas 1952, my father came down to Georgia, and we returned on that long train journey. I said goodbye to my friends, and we promised to meet in Vicksburg sometime in the distant future. I have no idea how long each of them stayed in Warm Springs or whatever happened to them.

★★★

Warm Springs jump-started my recovery, but it did lots of other things as well. For one thing, almost from day one I realized how fortunate I was compared to most of the other kids there. Any grounds for self-pity were eliminated. Second, I was impressed with a totally different view of President Roosevelt from what I was taught in Nashville. Pictures of Roosevelt were all over the place, and he was revered by practically everyone. Everything that I had heard about Roosevelt back home was bad. He was a socialist. He tried to nationalize the banks. He hated the South. He hated business. He tried to destroy our country, our way of life. He was a northern Democrat. Yet in Warm Springs I learned he pulled us out of the Great Depression. He put people back to work. He cared about the little guy. He fought the Japanese and Germans. How could there be such different opinions about one person? Which views were right? My experience in Warm Springs told me that he was not the evil person he was made out to be in the Nashville neighborhood I grew up in.

The images of the shantytowns scattered alongside the train tracks stayed in my mind for a long time. I concluded that Roosevelt must have really faced some tough problems because there still were a lot of poor people in this country and a lot of impoverished neighborhoods.

Given the times, Warm Springs was segregated. I do not recall many black staff, and the few there worked in the kitchen and did janitorial duties. As for the children, I saw no black polio victims at Warm Springs.

★★★

I returned home to balloons and a joyful celebration. Many of my friends came over, as they would dutifully for the next nine months that I remained out of school trying to get my muscles back. I went to physical therapy three days a week at Vanderbilt Hospital and got better and better. By the late spring of 1953 I was able to use my right hand to write.

I was able to keep up with my class by having a homebound teacher appointed by the public school system. She came to my house three mornings a week. She seemed nice enough, and I managed to keep up more or less without working very hard. The main thing I remember about her was a story she told me once, which she prefaced by saying it was horrible. The story was about a very prominent young woman who was married to a nice man, and everything was going just fine until she gave birth to their first child. It turned out the child was colored, "brown as a chestnut." I was somewhat puzzled and asked how that could be if the husband was white. "Nigger blood, that's what. He had Nigger blood in him." I was also puzzled as to why she thought this was the most horrible thing she had ever heard. When I asked what happened next, she said with an exasperated look on her face, "Well, of course, she divorced him. Immediately. And she put the child up for adoption. What else could she do?"

By the middle of the summer I had ditched the wheelchair and was able to do almost everything I could do before, albeit at a much lower level. I could walk but not run and could write barely legibly. I learned to use my left hand for practically everything besides writing. I had tried hard to make the switch to writing left-handed but just could not do it. I think I secretly wanted to show the doctor he was wrong. The doctors said I was ready to go back to school in the fall. I was overjoyed!

The 1953–54 school year was wonderful in many ways. I had a terrific sixth-grade teacher, Miss Brownlee. I made new friends and felt accepted for who I was. There was not much talk about polio or the fact that I could not do lots of things other kids could do. I think people went out of their way not to treat me differently, and for this I was grateful. Because I did not have much in the way of stomach muscles, I had to wear a corset to keep my back straight; but that was manageable. About halfway through the year the doctors thought a body cast would be better, so I had that put on and I managed that as well. I did have to take naps while my buddies gallivanted on the playground; but as the year progressed, I became part of the gang and found myself getting back to normal. I even had a girlfriend I had met at one of the church dances.

The next year was even better. I was back to my old self. Even though I had a body cast, I was able to do some athletics and was third string on the seventh-grade basketball team. A couple of times boys much bigger than me bumped into me, hit my body cast with their heads, and came away with a big headache. During football season I was the team manager, or "water boy." I continued to do well in school and loved my seventh-grade teacher, Mr. Bass, who endeared himself to the boys by bringing a TV to school and allowing the class to watch all of the World Series. I was even able to throw a baseball again with my right hand and arm, though admittedly I did not have my old stuff. I joined the Boy Scouts. I was active in my young people's group at

Christ Episcopal Church. I had plenty of friends. I was about as normal as you could get.

That is why I mark one day during the first week in June 1955 as among the darkest in my life. My mother and father asked me to join them in the living room and said that they had some news to share with me. They looked somber, and I concluded that the news was probably not good, but I had no hint of what they might be getting ready to tell me. My father did most of the talking. He said that they had been speaking to the doctors at Vanderbilt and that there were some problems with my back. My father explained that it seemed that I had developed "scoliosis," or curvature of the spine, because I did not have the muscle strength to help keep my back growing straight.

"So what does that mean?" I asked, holding my breath. I had no idea that there was anything wrong with my back. Sure, I wore a body cast, but no one had ever said anything about my backbone not growing properly.

"It means you will have to have an operation," my mother said, "so they can fix it and make it straight again."

I felt like an arrow had just pierced my heart.

"And how long is all this going to take?" I groaned. I could feel my body start to shake.

"Well, they are not sure, but it will mean you will be out of school for next year."

I heard the word "year" and bolted out of the room, running straight to my bedroom. I slammed the door as hard as I could and screamed at the top of my lungs, "Shit!"

Curse words were never used in our house; and except for an occasional "damn," I don't think I had ever heard my father swear. He had lectured me on occasion about using proper language, "especially around women."

"Well, I am in trouble now," I thought, "but so what?" Missing the next year of school was like a death sentence. I had worked so hard to be normal, to get back into the mainstream, to keep old friends and make new ones. And now this? Life was not fair, it was just not fair.

After a few minutes there was a knock on my door. It was my father. "It's all right, son, you are entitled to feel this way; and if I were you, I would feel exactly the same." He did not say a word about my foul language. He was carrying a large envelope, which he opened, and he pulled out large photo negative.

"I want you to look at this." It was an X-ray of my back. He held it up to the light.

I stared at the X-ray trying to figure out what it was and what it meant. It had a black background with a white skeleton image on it. I could make out shoulders and ribs. Where there would ordinarily have been a straight backbone, there was something looking like the letter "C." I was stunned.

"That's my backbone?" I asked.

"Yes," my father replied. "And the problem is that if they don't straighten it, your vital organs will get all out of whack and you probably will not live past twenty-one. But there is an operation that can fix it. It is called a spinal fusion where they go in and straighten out the backbone and then fuse something to your back that will keep it straight. The operation is quite new, but Vanderbilt is one of the places where it has been tried, and the success rate is above 50 percent."

Above 50 percent? Was that supposed to be good news or bad news?

"And what if it is not successful?"

"They will just have to do it again."

I continued staring at the X-ray. I then looked my father in the eye and said, "When can they do the operation?"

Chapter Three:
Separate and Unequal

B efore my operation, I came to breakfast one day and found my
father reading the morning paper more intently than usual as he
ate his bacon and eggs prepared by my mother. She was looking over his
shoulder and was as engaged as he was. I could feel the tension in the air
and moved closer to see what the paper said. There was a huge headline,
bigger than I had ever seen. It simply said, "Segregation Out." The day
was May 18, 1954. The Supreme Court had just ruled unanimously in
Brown v. Board of Education that school segregation was unconstitutional.
All the old rules were about to change.

While I had been aware that things were not exactly as they should
be based on my young sense of justice, at that time I did not really
understand what the term "segregation" meant. I knew that colored
kids and white kids did not go to the same schools or after a certain age
associate with each other. I also knew that there were sections of town
where colored people lived and where everyone seemed very poor.
This was just the way it was. It might not seem right, but what could
you do about it? If I had heard the word "segregation," I had never
fully realized that there was a legal system in place in the South which
enforced the separation of the races. Also, for the past two years I had
been focused on basically one thing—getting back on my feet and back
into the mainstream. That is why the first question I asked my parents
was, "What is segregation and what does this mean?"

My father looked up from his paper with a serious expression. He
did not seem to know what to say. After a long moment, he replied,

"Well, one thing it means is that colored children and white children now have to attend the same schools. It is not going to happen overnight, but it is now going to happen."

"Yes," my mother broke in, looking at me, "but it really is not going to affect you because we had always planned to send you to a private high school."

"And there will be other things as well," said my father. "It is too early to tell and it is all going to take a long time, but one thing is for sure, things will be different going forward. The South will never be the same again."

Was this a good thing or a bad thing? I searched for clues in my parents' faces. I honestly could not tell. I got my courage up and asked directly, "Is this good or bad?"

"It's just different," my father said. "Let's leave it at that."

★★★

While May 17, 1954, marked the official end of legally sanctioned school segregation in the United States, efforts to change the system had been going on for some time. The first civil rights organization—the National Association for the Advancement of Colored People (NAACP)—was founded in 1909 with a national office in New York City. The founders included sixty people, mostly white liberals from the North, several of whom were the children of abolitionists. Only seven of the original sixty were African American, but that ratio changed quickly as the organization grew. The goal of the organization was to assure that the Thirteenth, Fourteenth, and Fifteenth Amendments to the Constitution were observed in practice, and its focus was on the Jim Crow laws in the South and school segregation everywhere. An early leader at the NAACP was Charles Houston, dean of the Howard University Law School. He later recruited Thurgood Marshall, who spearheaded the effort to overturn *Plessy v. Ferguson,* the U.S. Supreme Court decision that in 1896 upheld segregation. After many years of planning and careful strategy, they were finally successful in *Brown v. Board of Education of Topeka.*

Up until that time, there had been limited organized effort to overturn segregation in the United States. Three other national groups focused on civil rights issues. The oldest of these was the National Urban League, a New York–based advocacy organization formed in the merger of several groups in 1910. The second group was the Congress of Racial Equality (CORE), an outgrowth of the Christian pacifist Fellowship of Reconciliation. CORE had been founded in the early 1940s to focus on grassroots organizational and economic justice racial issues; but until *Brown v. Board of Education*, the organization hadn't had a high profile. Founded by James Farmer and George Hauser, CORE had organized an integrated bus ride through the South in 1947—the "Journey of Reconciliation"—which got considerable publicity; but CORE had not accomplished anything else of this magnitude. The third group, the Brotherhood of Sleeping Car Porters, founded in 1935 by A. Philip Randolph, was the first African American–led trade union. No other significant civil rights organizations were operating in the late 1950s.

There had also been intellectual centers of social activism, such as the Highlander Folk School in the mountains of East Tennessee and Koinonia Farm in Sumter County in southwest Georgia. The Highlander Folk School was founded in 1932, in the depths of the Great Depression, for the purpose of organizing labor in the South. In the 1950s it turned its attention to civil rights and became a training ground for civil rights leaders like Martin Luther King Jr. Koinonia Farm, founded in 1942 as a religious haven championing justice and peace causes, in the 1950s turned its attention to Jim Crow and poverty. While neither of these institutions engaged in direct action or mass protest, both were influential in developing the early leadership of the civil rights movement.

One of the people who attended workshops at the Highlander Folk School in Tennessee was Rosa Parks. At the age of forty-two she was secretary of the Montgomery, Alabama, chapter of the NAACP. She had been carefully recruited to protest the segregated bus system in Montgomery. The workshop she attended introduced the idea of nonviolent civil disobedience to address issues of segregation in the South. Not long after she returned home—on December 1, 1955—a white person got on the bus she was riding and asked her to move. She didn't. She was immediately arrested, tried, and put in jail.

The president of the Montgomery chapter of the NAACP was Edgar Daniel Nixon, known as E. D. Nixon. He was also the leader of the local branch of the Brotherhood of Sleeping Car Porters, and he had been involved in several small protests in Montgomery during the preceding years. Nixon was looking for someone to challenge the bus ordinance in

Montgomery and had selected Parks among three candidates. Working with Nixon was Jo Ann Robinson, another member of the NAACP and a member of the Women's Political Council. A college professor at Alabama State College, she had been abused by white bus drivers on previous occasions. The day after Parks's arrest, E. D. Nixon provided bail, and Jo Ann Robinson stayed up all night mimeographing thirty-five thousand handbills. The handbills were distributed to ministers and to high school students and called for a one-day boycott of the bus system.

Nixon called African American pastors in Montgomery to try to find someone who would head up the effort. One of the pastors he talked to was Ralph Abernathy, and he and Nixon formed the Montgomery Improvement Association (MIP) to oversee the boycott. There was also a young minister named Martin Luther King Jr., who had recently moved to Montgomery, having just received his PhD from Boston University. Nixon asked him if he would support the boycott. King said that he would, but they still needed a leader. In trying to organize the clergy, Nixon, to his dismay, encountered considerable resistance among the black clergy, most of whom argued for a go-slow approach, avoiding any direct confrontation with the white power structure and business community. King was new to the area, had little experience dealing with the white community, and was more eager than most to participate. When in a heated meeting Nixon denounced the clergy as a bunch of cowards, King stood up and protested that *he* was no coward; and before the meeting was over, he was elected president of the MIP. Abernathy was elected second in command as program director. Martin Luther King Jr. was twenty-six years old.

The boycott was more effective than anyone could have imagined, lasting 381 days, ending on December 21, 1956, with the local bus operation virtually bankrupt. The boycott ended when the U.S. Supreme Court ruled that the Montgomery segregation policy was unlawful. The protest had been a huge success, placed the race issue in a spotlight in the news media, and gotten America's attention. The civil rights movement had begun. And it had found a leader.

In anticipation of the boycott idea's spreading to other cities, the leaders of the Montgomery boycott decided to expand the structure of the MIP. A conference was held in Atlanta in mid-January 1957 to bring together black leaders from throughout the South and develop a civil rights strategy going forward. Some sixty people attended from ten states. Even though Ralph Abernathy's house was bombed during the conference, the meeting continued. They named the new organization the Southern Christian Leadership Conference on Transportation and Nonviolent Integration. The name was soon shortened to the Southern Christian Leadership Conference (SCLC). King was elected president and Abernathy, financial secretary–treasurer. The organization declared that "civil rights are essential to democracy, that segregation must end, and that all black people must reject segregation absolutely and nonviolently."

The ending of the Montgomery boycott made the front pages of most papers but was soon overshadowed by what was happening in Arkansas. In October 1957 Arkansas Governor Orval Faubus called out the state national guard to prevent school desegregation from happening in that state. I remember watching that drama on television when President Eisenhower called in the 101st Airborne Division from Fort Campbell, Kentucky, and federalized Faubus's National Guard. I also remember seeing the frightened looks on the faces of the black students walking past an angry mob of white hecklers shouting racial epithets as they tried to enter Little Rock High School. It was an ugly picture, and I wondered how anyone looking at it could side with the mob.

These two incidents both occurred when I was trying to get back on my feet from polio. They were far from Nashville and did not affect me personally in any way. But at the same time I was shocked and haunted by what I had seen on television and wondered what would be happening next.

Chapter Four:

Down but Not Out

The spinal fusion operation was scheduled for early July 1955. I played hard with my friends the few weeks preceding the operation thinking they might well be my last opportunity to play tag or throw a baseball. The operation involved opening up my back, straightening my backbone, and then fusing a bone shaving from my shin onto my backbone to give it more strength. The main thing I remember when I regained consciousness was how severe the pain was all over my body and how good the drugs were. I could understand why people became drug addicts. The doctors announced that the operation was a success as far as it went but warned that I would have to remain flat (on my back or stomach) for at least six months; and under no circumstances could my back be elevated more than six inches. They would not be able to declare the operation a real success until they could evaluate how I was doing in six months.

The period from July 1955 to July 1956—my eighth-grade year— was in many ways much like the 1952–53 year—my fifth-grade year. I was assigned a homebound teacher, a pleasant woman who did not seem to have the racist tendencies of my first homebound teacher. The next year I was supposed to attend high school, and I wondered if I actually was learning anything. I later concluded that the answer to this question was probably no, but that the kids in school were not learning much either, because when I did return I was not far behind my friends. One thing this teacher did was to encourage me to write. She sent in one of my essays to the other local newspaper, the *Nashville Tennessean*.

It was about why some teenagers go bad and some don't; and to my astonishment and pleasure, it was published as an op-ed.

Most of my friends stuck with me during this period, as they had the first time; there was hardly an afternoon that someone did not come over to visit me. My first girlfriend visited regularly, though when I got back on my feet I learned that she had a healthy boyfriend as well. There is no way to overstate how important it was to have those friends come over. They kept me in touch with what was going on; and every morning when I was mostly alone, I would anxiously await the afternoon visits. We would listen to music, play Monopoly or Risk or electric football or chess or just talk about what was happening in the world beyond my house.

The other thing that kept me going was the radio. This was the year I discovered rhythm and blues. I can't remember who turned me on to this music, but it was not long before I was listening to "clear channel" WLAC every night. The John R Show came on at 8:00 followed by the Gene Nobles Show from 9:00 to 11:00. The Gene Nobles Show was my favorite. Both John R (actually John Richburg) and Gene Nobles were white, but the music they played was exclusively black, and both shows had listeners tuning in from all over the South. The major sponsors were White Rose Petroleum Jelly, Royal Crown Stick Pomade, and Randy's Record Shop. Periodically a Tarzan-like yell would come on, and Gene Nobles would say something like, "Way to go, Cohort, you like that song, do you!" As soon as a new song was released, it would be played on his show. Almost every night there was at least one new release. I heard brand new songs from artists like Fats Domino, Big Joe Turner, Etta James, the Drifters, Little Richard, the Coasters, the Platters, Bo Didley, Guitar Slim, and Chuck Berry. I loved this music and could not get enough of it. I would place my clunky tape recorder—a relatively new invention at the time—next to the radio, record the tune, and then the next day ask my father to pick up the record at Ernie's Record Shop in downtown Nashville. I often wondered what they must have thought of this straight-laced, white banker in a dark suit coming into Ernie's two or three times a week and buying the first copies of songs—all by black artists—that turned out to be number one hits. My father did say someone asked him once which record company he represented. If I still had my record collection today, it would be worth a fortune.

I considered myself Gene Nobles's greatest fan. Since I listened to the show every night, I figured no one listened any more than me. And I wrote fan letter after fan letter. I drew pictures of what I thought

"Cohort" looked like (a green giant), I told him which artists I liked best (Chuck Berry and the Drifters), I commented on some of the things he talked about on the show, and I made my own special requests for songs. Every night he would read several fan letters and usually play their requests but never one of mine. I figured that if I kept writing, one of these days he would have to read it on the air, but it never happened. Eventually I gave up and stopped writing fan letters, resigning myself to this as another that's-just-the-way-the-world-is situation.

This is why a day in the spring of 1956 will go down as one of the best in my life. That evening I was listening as I always did, recording the new songs, and not thinking much about it when Gene Nobles came on and said that the next song was dedicated to a very special person who was recovering from polio. Well, I thought, this is interesting: someone else out there besides me has polio and is into R&B music. (I was careful never to mention polio in any of my fan letters.) He went on to say that the person was twelve years old and was "convalescing" from a back operation, and just as I thought the coincidence was impossible, Gene Nobles said, "This goes out to my number one fan, Joe Howell, and we all wish him a speedy recovery!"

It was like I had just won the lottery. I let out a big whoop of joy. Within seconds my door opened, and there were my father and mother, beaming and looking very pleased with themselves, along with two dinner guests, one of whom was a radio executive who knew Gene Nobles. So that's how it happened, I realized. It was not my guardian angel who arranged this, and yet for me it was a miracle nonetheless.

So one of the main events of the second year of recovery was my discovery of black music. What was this bond I felt with the music and with the artists? In some way my passion for the music and for the people who created it led to my identification with black people struggling for freedom, but this would come much later, not until I reached college. Yet I believe this was another seed that was planted, another one of those unexpected blessings.

A second important thing that happened during that year was that for the first time I got to know Emma Hammerick, our maid, not as a servant but as a real human being. Since my mother was out a lot running errands and going to meetings, Emma and I were often in the house alone together. She had worked for my parents for as long as I could remember, and to a twelve-year-old she seemed ageless. While she was considerably older than either of my parents, she lived to be 103, outliving my mother.

When I started playing one of my favorite rhythm and blues records, I could see her eyes sparkle; and often she would start to swing with the music. As we got to talking I discovered that she loved all the artists I loved. She suggested new artists that I should keep an eye on. I should not have been amazed, but I was. Perhaps even more impressive was that she was just as avid a baseball fan as I was and personally knew Roy Campanella, the legendary catcher of the Brooklyn Dodgers. The Dodgers had won the World Series the year before in 1955, and in the summer of 1956 Emma was able to get me a baseball signed by every member of that world champion Dodger team. Years later my three-year-old son would deposit the ball into the toilet, an action which resulted in all the names being washed away. A second fortune lost.

A third blessing had to do with religion. My parents were both involved in the downtown Episcopal church in various leadership positions, and I attended Sunday school, served as an acolyte, and was president of our preteen youth group. The church was somewhat diverse, attracting people from all parts of Nashville, including a lot of Vanderbilt professors. There were no black people in the congregation at Christ Church, but the clergy had a history of being progressive on social issues, and there was no pushback on the *Brown* decision as there was in so many churches in Nashville.

There was a lot I liked about Christ Church, but I came very close to going a different route. Most of my friends went to Southern Baptist churches, and I had attended a few of these services from time to time. One of my best neighborhood friends was Walter Wilson, whose family was Southern Baptist. In the spring of 1954, during that period between my sixth- and seventh-grade years before my operation when I was getting back to normal, the Billy Graham Crusade came to Nashville, and it was a big deal. Though Graham was a Southern Baptist, the crusade was billed as nondenominational, and my parents were involved in recruiting Episcopalians. Our attendance at the crusade was a command performance, and I got to bring along one friend. I brought Walter.

All the planning effort paid off, and the Vanderbilt football stadium was packed with more than fifty thousand white people in anxious anticipation of hearing the Gospel preached by one of the greatest preachers of all time. Graham did not disappoint. When the call came to come down on the field and repent of your sins and be forgiven, I could not resist. I looked at Walter and Walter looked at me. I nodded. He nodded. Down we went.

The problem was that Walter and I were seated on the very top row of the stadium, since we did not want to sit with my parents in the VIP section. They had reluctantly agreed to let us sit up there. But to get to the stage in the center of the football stadium we had to walk down the steps past the VIP section, which was about two-thirds of the way down to the field. I didn't think twice about it until I happened to catch a glimpse of my mother out of the corner of my eye as she was looking over her shoulder. There was suddenly a horrified look on her face as our eyes met. I knew something was not right. A moment later, just before Walter and I passed by their row, I started to charge down the stairs. Suddenly a hand grabbed me and pulled me down into a vacant seat. It was my father. Walter had a surprised look on his face, then he stopped and squeezed in beside me. There was a collective moan coming from all around us, and several people shouted, "Let them go, let them go!" Someone shouted, "Jesus saves." Someone else muttered, "Satan." I looked down at my feet and wished I were dead.

"What's wrong with going down there?" I feebly asked when I got my wits about me. My mother whispered to me sternly, almost in a stage whisper, "What is wrong is that *those* people are Southern Baptists and *you* are an Episcopalian, and you don't *need* to be saved. You are the president of Christ Church Preteen Youth Group. For goodness sakes!"

Neither Walter nor I said much after that, and there never was any further discussion about the event with my parents.

I am not sure that if I had been saved I would have necessarily become a Southern Baptist; but since I was not saved, it was not an issue, and I never left the Episcopal Church. It turned out that sticking with Christ Church was a good thing, because several clergy there meant a lot to me during both times I was homebound. On average I got a visit every two or three weeks and enjoyed talking to them about various topics, most not directly associated with religion—sports, rock 'n' roll, school, TV programs, and activities going on at church.

One clergyman stopped by more often than the others. Soon after I returned home from the hospital, he gave me a book of meditations and prayers and said, "Joe, I know that this is difficult for you and that the next year will not be easy, but in some ways you actually are very lucky. You will have the gift of solitude and silence and will have the opportunity to talk with God in ways that are not available to your friends. Read these prayers and meditations and keep your ears open, and you will be greatly rewarded."

In mysterious ways he was right. I never felt closer to God than I did in those days. I felt loved, and I felt that through God's love I would come through my ordeal with polio. Because of this feeling and because of the love shown to me by the clergy at Christ Church, I got the notion that someday I would become an Episcopal priest. There was also a seed that was planted in those days of silence and solitude, a feeling that God cares about *all* people—people like me who had polio or some other disability and people who did not live in fancy homes or have a lot of money, people who were white like me and people who were colored like Emma.

★★★

By summer of 1956, the doctors officially proclaimed the operation a success. I was finally allowed to sit up. The whole world appeared different. I had gotten used to viewing everything from a prone position. Everything now looked smaller. I started physical therapy again, this time to help me relearn how to walk. How could you forget how to walk? It took several weeks of hard physical therapy for my legs to remember what to do. I still had to wear a body cast, which would be with me for a couple of more years, but the recovery was much quicker than before; and by the end of the summer I was ready to reenter the mainstream.

My mother had promised that I would not be impacted by the *Brown* decision because I would be going to a private high school. The original order seeking desegregation of the Nashville school system was filed in 1955, but no desegregation of any significance would happen for more than fifteen years. None of the white public high schools allowed black students to attend while I was in high school, and it seemed on the surface that during that period Nashville was untouched by the *Brown* decision. However, fear of integration was not the reason they were sending me to a private high school. I was going to a private high school because the private high school they selected for me, the city's premier private high school, Montgomery Bell Academy (MBA), was where sons from families like mine went. I loved the place. I was coming out of another year of isolation and needed a caring environment with structure and order. It was small, with about two hundred students, fewer than fifty students per class; and several of my classmates were already my friends. MBA was a day school but had the culture of a classic prep school. Tradition was important. Values were important.

The school motto was "Gentleman, scholar, athlete." Teachers were excellent and committed to learning and to students. Most spent their entire career there. The headmaster was steeped in "the prep school ethos" and instilled "the MBA spirit" and pride in most of us.

What really made MBA special for me, however, was my athletic experience. While I was not able to play sports, I could be a "team manager," responsible for doing whatever needed to be done to be sure practices ran smoothly and the players were ready for the games, so I became the student manager of the junior varsity football team my freshman year. My second year at MBA a new position was created called "student athletic trainer," and the head football coach, Tommy Owen, asked me if I would like to fill it. I immediately said yes, and I spent most of the summer reading manuals about wrapping ankles, taping knees, and learning fundamental anatomy. By the time summer football practice rolled around, I was ready to go. For the next three years I was the official student trainer for football, basketball, and track, earning as many sports letters as anyone in my class. I taped ankles before games, gave rubdowns, carried water to the football players during timeouts, wrapped knees, gave encouragement to the players, and kept the shot chart during basketball games.

The best side benefit of being the student trainer was the relationship I developed with Coach Owen, one of the school's most successful and popular coaches. Besides being a great coach, he was a man with integrity who had a genuine love for his players. Since both of us often worked late hours in the locker room, I had a chance to get to know him better than many of his athletes, and he became almost a second father.

For me, MBA was a godsend. Not only was it my ticket back into the mainstream, it provided me with self-confidence and a sense of self-worth. I studied hard, did well in class, made lots of new friends, some of whom remain close friends to this day, and felt appreciated for my work as a student trainer. I was elected to various class officer positions and became a student leader. I joined a fraternity and was part of the in-crowd. It could not have been much better.

But as hard as I tried, I never quite made it completely back into the mainstream. This all was driven home to me when I attended Boys State the summer before my senior year. Boys State was a week-long event held throughout the United States that focused on good government and civics. Boys finishing their junior year of high school were nominated for the program by their school administrators. I was honored to have been chosen by my headmaster and was looking forward to meeting other student leaders from all over Tennessee—only white boys, of course, a fact of life that was not questioned. I got into the spirit of things and ran for various offices as we were all supposed to do.

Every morning the entire group of more than one thousand student leaders gathered on the football field for calisthenics and athletic competition—softball, volleyball, basketball, and various other sports. I struggled to participate in most activities without hurting my teams. One day toward the end of the week, the leader of the calisthenics was a notorious drill sergeant, an ex-Marine who on several occasions had announced that our generation was a "bunch of pussies." We lined up on the field and started our push-ups and sit-ups as he meandered through the crowd monitoring how we were doing. As he strolled past, he paused and stared at me. This was during the sit-up phase, which I would simply sit out because I had no stomach muscles. I did not make eye contact with him but could feel him glaring at me as I watched my fellow participants go through their routines. I could feel myself blushing.

All of a sudden he took his microphone, which was connected to the loudspeakers on the football field, and screamed, "Everybody stop. Stop right now." There was an abrupt pause in activity and an eerie silence.

He looked down at me as his voice boomed out over the loudspeakers, "What is your name, son, and where are you from?" He thrust the mike in my face.

I knew trouble was coming but mustered the courage to mutter grimly, "My name is Joe Howell and I am from Nashville and attend Montgomery Bell Academy."

"OK," he bellowed. "Now do a sit-up."

I could feel the eyes of one thousand boys all looking straight at me.

"A sit-up?" I asked feebly, trying to buy some time.

"Are you deaf, boy? Any fool can do a sit-up, now just do one."

Well, I thought, I really haven't tried to do a sit-up recently, maybe if I try real hard . . .

I tried—and failed, then failed again and again. I could hear a collective gasp from one thousand boys.

"Now this is an example of what I have been talking about all week! What is your name, son? Joe Howell? This 'Joe Howell from Montgomery Bell Academy' is an example of what a bunch of milk toasts and pussies you boys are. You think you are some kind of big deal, but this kid can't even do a sit-up. Pitiful, just pitiful." He moved on, and the sit-ups started up again, while I looked desperately for a hole to climb in.

Despite the Boys State experience, my high school years were good years for me, although I had the notion that everything was not perfect. It was as if we were living an idyllic life in a kind of Garden of Eden surrounded by a larger world with a lot of pain. There were the usual inspirational speeches in assembly about honor and integrity and doing the right thing—and I believed all of that—but those values often seemed confined to the MBA campus and our own small world. What about what was going on beyond our campus?

This question haunted me, especially when I was involved in social service outreach efforts to "those less fortunate." Every year my fraternity had social service projects, delivering a turkey to a needy family at Thanksgiving and delivering toys to poor families at Christmas. I usually volunteered to help, but the experience depressed me. I felt guilty about being depressed. After all we were doing a good deed. The other guys seemed to feel good about themselves, while I seemed to identify with the poor families. I could feel the pain of what I thought they must be feeling. At the time I could not figure out why I felt this way, but now I link it to the pain I felt when I was confined to a bed and had no assurance I would ever be able to get back on my feet and be like everyone else.

The needy families we were helping usually lived in houses similar to the shotgun shacks that I visited when I went fundraising with my mother and when looking out of the window of the train to Atlanta. They were both African American and white. One family in particular stands out. The mother, probably in her early thirties, was a white woman who lived near the Tennessee State Penitentiary. She was completely bedraggled. Four or five half-naked, dirt-streaked kids were running wild around her living room, which had practically no furniture. There was no rug on the floor and no pictures on the wall. One of the window panes was broken. Two junked cars sat in the front yard. Trash was everywhere. The young mother was so grateful when we delivered the turkey she had to wipe tears from her eyes. I had the same feeling of embarrassment I had when my mother and I were collecting money for the orphanage. Life should not be this hard for some people. Bringing the family a turkey for Thanksgiving was fine, but what about the other 364 days of the year? Why were things this way?

Chapter Five:

Change Begins

Though we white boys at MBA remained insulated and unaware, the racial order was being challenged behind the scenes all over the South in the late 1950s, and in no place more than Nashville.

Kelly Miller Smith was pastor of the black First Baptist Church on Capitol Hill, only blocks from the shantytown that had made such an impression on me. Originally from Mississippi and with degrees from Morehouse and Howard, he moved to Nashville in 1951 and became the head of the Nashville chapter of the NAACP in 1958, my sophomore year in high school. Reverend Smith was impressed with the Montgomery bus boycott and established the Nashville Christian Leadership Council (NCLC) as an affiliate of SCLC.

In March 1958 the NCLC began to sponsor a series of workshops on nonviolent civil disobedience. Nonviolence was the cornerstone of the early civil rights philosophy and strategy. Smith had struck up a relationship with a thirty-year-old Vanderbilt Divinity School student named James Lawson. Vanderbilt's graduate programs for the most part had desegregated in the late 1950s, and Lawson was among the first African American students. He was from Pennsylvania and had attended college in the North. He had become involved in the Fellowship of Reconciliation, the interfaith pacifist organization, and in CORE, the early civil rights group that promoted civil disobedience. He had served jail time for his pacifist views, and as a Methodist missionary in India he had become interested in the teachings of Mohandas Gandhi. While there he attended classes and workshops on Gandhi's principles of nonviolence. Martin Luther King Jr., who shared this interest, had requested Lawson's help during the Montgomery bus boycott, and the two became good friends.

The workshops conducted in 1958 and in 1959 attracted a large following, mainly from the major historically black colleges and universities in Nashville—Fisk, Tennessee A&I, American Baptist Theological Seminary, and Meharry Medical College. Several people who would later play leadership roles in the civil rights movement were involved—John Lewis, Marion Barry, John Bevel, Diane Nash, and C. T. Vivian, among others. Out of the workshops emerged a written code of ethics that dictated behavior during sit-ins and demonstrations, which emphasized discipline, the teachings of Jesus and Gandhi, and the principle of nonviolence.

By the end of 1959 Kelly Miller Smith's organization had targeted segregated lunch counters as logical places to begin and put plans in place for sit-ins if the lunch counters refused to allow blacks to eat beside whites. Smith and Lawson met with the owners of the two large department stores in Nashville, Fred Harvey and John Sloan. Both men refused to integrate their lunch counters, and NCLS staged test sit-ins on November 28 at Harvey's and on December 5 at Cain-Sloan. There were only a few participants involved, and the sit-ins got no press coverage. The response at Harvey's was later described as relatively polite, the reaction at Cain-Sloan, hostile. Based on this reconnaissance effort, plans began for a much higher profile engagement.

Neither I nor practically anyone else in white Nashville had any idea this was going on or what was going to happen next.

The next sit-in in Nashville took place on February 13, 1960. This one was the real thing. Nashville was not the first site of a high-profile lunch counter sit-in, however. Two weeks earlier, on February 1, four African American students from North Carolina A&T took seats at the lunch counter at Woolworth's department store in downtown Greensboro. Up until then blacks could stand and order food but not sit down. The manager took a hands-off approach at first; but when the students did not leave, he called the police, who monitored the situation but did not arrest anyone. The next day the same four students reappeared with twenty-seven others, including students from Bennett College and Dudley High School as well as more A&T students. Within days the number of protestors had risen to three hundred. White mobs gathered to jeer, and bomb threats forced the manager to close the entire store for over two weeks beginning February 6. The event got major coverage in both local and national media. The movement quickly spread to other cities in the South.

Nashville was city number two. Just after noon on Saturday, February 13, 1960, 124 students, most but not all black, simultaneously walked into three downtown department stores and asked to be seated at the lunch counters. When they were refused, they sat down anyway, then left two hours later without incident. Two days later, on Monday, February 15, the black Baptist Ministers Conference of Nashville issued a statement saying that they supported the sit-ins and asked all people of goodwill to boycott Nashville stores which practiced segregation. The battle lines had been drawn.

Over the next two weeks, there were three more sit-ins in Nashville. Each new demonstration added more participants, and new stores were added to the list. Angry white mobs appeared; but for the most part the police monitored the situation, and there was no violence. Demonstrators would remain for two or three hours, then retreat to one of the Baptist churches for a rally. The third demonstration, however, turned ugly. For some reason the police were not present. The white mob attacked the black participants. Several demonstrators were beaten; one was thrown down the stairs. When the police arrived, the white attackers dispersed, and the police ordered the black protestors to leave. When they refused, the police made eighty-one arrests for disorderly conduct and loitering. It made the headlines of all the local newspapers and the wires of the Associated Press. I read about all this in the Nashville papers, but in some ways it seemed almost as far away from Belle Meade and MBA as Little Rock or Montgomery.

The trial took place on February 29. More than two thousand people lined the streets around the Nashville courthouse in support of the demonstrators. The students were represented by thirteen lawyers, headed by Z. Alexander Looby, a prominent black attorney and Fisk University professor. The judge found the demonstrators guilty and fined them each fifty dollars. They all refused to pay and were sent to jail for thirty-five days. On April 19, shortly after the students' release, Looby's house was dynamited and almost destroyed, though miraculously no one was hurt. A subsequent rally drew more than four thousand supporters of the sit-ins. When Vanderbilt University got wind of Lawson's role in the demonstrations, he was ordered by the Vanderbilt Executive Committee to cease all involvement in them. He refused and was immediately expelled from the Vanderbilt Divinity School. Blacks began a boycott of Nashville stores. Martin Luther King visited Fisk and praised the demonstrators. The sit-ins continued, and more than 150 demonstrators were arrested and jailed. Nashville was in the headlines throughout the United States.

All this was going on during my senior year in high school. I would like to report that I was on the frontlines and a participant in the sit-ins, or at least one of the few white supporters, and that I understood what an injustice segregation was and how white people needed to stand up to end it. But for some reason I was not able to connect the dots. For one thing it all seemed to happen without warning. There had been anxiety following the Supreme Court decision about what desegregation would mean to Nashville, and then for more than five years nothing changed. White Nashville became complacent. We fell back into business as usual. The other thing I find puzzling is that I do not have a better recollection of the details of what was going on in downtown Nashville during my final semester at MBA. I knew that there were sit-ins and arrests, but it is almost as though I wanted to pretend they were not happening. They were someone else's problem.

How could a young person like me, who was appalled by witnessing poverty in both black and white poor neighborhoods in Nashville and who by nature tended to identify with the little guy, fail to understand the significance of what was going on and get behind it? That question could be asked of a lot of well-intentioned white people who like me must have known deep down that institutional and legal racism were wrong. We lacked either the wisdom or the courage to understand this consciously. In my case it was probably both, but in time that would change.

A compromise was eventually reached in the Nashville sit-in crisis. The mayor of Nashville at the time was Ben West, who was progressive by southern standards of the day. After discussions with supporters of the demonstrators led by Kelly Smith, James Lawson, and other black ministers, West set up a biracial commission to study the situation and make recommendations. What it finally came up with in May 1960 was an agreement that for several weeks a small number of African Americans would be allowed to sit in the whites-only section of lunch counters one day each week. Store management would know beforehand when this would happen and attempt to minimize any disruption. The press was asked not to overplay the situation. After the breaking-in period, there would be no more restrictions. The plan went off without a hitch, and Nashville became the first southern city to desegregate private eating establishments. A few other cities would follow, but it would not be until the Civil Rights Act of 1964, which outlawed segregation of many varieties, that blacks and whites would be able to eat side by side in most southern cities.

The sit-ins marked the end of the second chapter of the civil rights movement. The excitement and publicity generated in Greensboro and Nashville inspired people in many other cities in the border states, such as North Carolina, Virginia, and Tennessee, to do the same. Protests were held in Winston-Salem; Raleigh; Durham; Charlotte; Richmond; Chattanooga; Atlanta; and Lexington, Kentucky. The term "sit-in" became a household word in America. Protests began to include public libraries, swimming pools, and public theaters. What began as a statement by four brave A&T university students had become a national movement.

★★★

One of the veteran civil rights activists in 1960 was Ella Baker. She was then fifty-seven years old and had been involved in various human-rights causes. Born in Norfolk, Virginia, she earned a degree from Shaw University and lived most of her adult life in New York City, where for much of the time she was the highest-ranking woman in the NAACP. When the Montgomery bus boycott took place, she traveled to Montgomery, where she became a friend of Martin Luther King Jr. and joined SCLC. She then moved to Atlanta to work in the SCLC office, mainly on voter registration. Following the Greensboro sit-ins she persuaded SCLC to fund a student leadership conference over Easter weekend at Shaw University in Raleigh. Black college students from all over the South attended the conference. They formed a new organization and called it the Student Nonviolent Coordinating Committee, or SNCC. Ella Baker left her imprint on the attendees. She complained that the civil rights movement had too few women, too many clergy, and was too leader-centered. SNCC adopted her notion of "participatory democracy" and grassroots organizing and would add a new dimension to the civil rights movement.

Attending the Raleigh conference in April 1960 were more than one hundred student delegates from some fifty-eight sit-in sites in twelve southern states and representatives from nineteen northern colleges and universities. Also represented were SCLC, CORE, the Fellowship of Reconciliation (FOR), the National Student Association (NSA), and Students for a Democratic Society (SDS). The names of people who attended are a who's who of future civil rights leaders, many of whom maintained high profiles in their subsequent careers. Among them were John Lewis, who became a congressman from Georgia; Julian Bond, a legislator from Georgia and chairman of the NAACP; and Marion Barry, the mayor of Washington, D.C.; among others. Several of the Nashville organizers were there as well, including James Lawson and Diane Nash. One of the SNCC founders in attendance was Charles Sherrod, the person who would recruit Embry and me six years later to join him and my fellow seminary students in southwest Georgia.

After SNCC was formed in the spring of 1960 there was a brief pause in the action. Maybe people were catching their breath, because the following year, 1961, would be one of the most important in the history of the movement.

Chapter Six:

College Years

At the time I had no idea about the formation of SNCC in Raleigh or the civil rights activities going on behind the scenes in Nashville, let alone the rest of the South. My goal in the spring of 1960 was to graduate from high school and attend a good college. I was accepted into Davidson College, a Presbyterian, all-men's school of one thousand students located about twenty miles north of Charlotte, North Carolina. My preference as a high school senior, which looking back on it seems odd, was to attend a college that was all male, small, liberal arts, affiliated with a religious denomination—and in the South. Davidson met these criteria and was a great school for me, but in ways I never would have expected.

While I was at Davidson, the civil rights movement came of age. You could not open a newspaper or turn on a television without being confronted with images of what was happening in race relations. Black churches were bombed; civil rights workers were murdered; innocent black people were leveled by water blasting from firemen's hoses, German shepherds nipping at their feet; National Guard units were mobilized; and innocent people were thrown in jail. It seemed that the country—or at least the South—was in the midst of a revolution. These images—conveyed daily on television and the newspaper—soaked in slowly, and eventually they reached me.

While my awareness of human suffering dated back to my brief encounters with abject poverty in the Nashville ghetto on my mother's fundraising efforts and to the long hours alone in my room during my bout with polio, that awareness grew in the summer of 1960. That summer before I entered college I spent three months working in a small village in the mountains of central Mexico. About a dozen Nashville high school graduating seniors piled into an old school bus painted pea green with the inscription *El Perro Verde* ("The Green Dog") on the side. About a week later—after several breakdowns—we pulled up to a small, dusty compound in a tiny village more than a mile above sea level. Two young Episcopal clergymen were our leaders, assisted by a nurse, an interpreter who was a U.S. college student from Mexico, and a bus driver. That summer our job was renovating an old church building and "assisting the Episcopal Church in Mexico." Our mandate may have involved some evangelism; but, because few of us spoke much Spanish, our main activities with the children of the village were playing soccer and baseball.

Again I confronted poverty but in a different way. While the villagers were very poor, many not having access to electricity or indoor plumbing, the situation did not seem as appalling as the shantytowns in Nashville. People were friendly, proud, and seemed to lead full lives. Yet there was no way to avoid the awareness of the vast difference in living conditions between where I grew up and where I was working that summer. Through the examples provided by the two clergy who led the effort, I came to understand the role the church could play in addressing social issues, and I came even closer to God.

I did not dwell on these questions about social inequities for too long, however. I returned to the States ready to go to college and feeling pretty good about our efforts.

★★★

One of the things I looked forward to most about going to college was being away from home. I would not know many people and at last could shed the image of the polio kid and be part of the mainstream. This all came together for me at Davidson. It was a fresh start. My first three and a half years at Davidson I did everything I was supposed to do. I joined a fraternity. I studied hard. I attended the tiny St. Alban's Episcopal Church on Sunday mornings. I did not engage in excessive partying. I went on road trips to nearby girls' colleges for blind dates and dances. One such visit to a Virginia woman's college led to my romance with and eventual marriage to Embry Martin (known in Davidson by her nickname, "Mimy"). I visited professors at open houses on Sunday evenings. I did social service work and became president of the student YMCA. This relatively conventional behavior placed me—along with a good number of my friends—in the category of a "drone," someone who was not cool.

Part of what made Davidson the right college for me was the extraordinary faculty of men dedicated to their fields and to their students. First among these for me was an eccentric and controversial English professor. "Doctor G," as we all called him, was in his early fifties. He was short and stout, with a square jaw, jowls, gray temples, and short hair. Usually disheveled, he always seemed to be carrying a stack of books and papers as he hurried to a class. He was a bachelor, and his whole life was teaching. His classes were only part of the picture. He would routinely take his favorite students to one of the beer joints in nearby towns (Davidson was "dry") for more discussions about what we were studying or experiencing. Doctor G's passion for literature, learning, and creativity inspired many students at Davidson, and some of us became his protégés. He challenged us with his sense of justice and his moral outrage at what was wrong with the world. He ranted and raved against nuclear weapons, Republicans, Davidson College trustees, the Presbyterian Church, tenure (which he did not have), third world poverty, censorship of the press, fraternities at Davidson, student complacency, and numerous other ills. One of these ills was racial prejudice and discrimination. He encouraged his disciples to make a difference, to get involved, and to fight injustice of all types on all fronts and not to give up. At times he would go too far, with lectures sounding more like sermons; but it was hard for Doctor G's fervor not to sink in. For me it brought into focus and confirmed many of the concerns I had about social injustice.

Slowly we became aware that changes were in the wind. The sit-ins in Greensboro had made the news; and in the fall of 1961, my sophomore year, the Freedom Riders showed up at Davidson College.

The Freedom Riders were en route to Alabama and Mississippi. There was not much publicity about their arrival, only a poster or two saying that they were passing through Davidson and would be available at the student union for questions and answers. Not knowing what they were all about, I was curious and decided to attend. When I arrived at the union, a dozen or so people were seated in a room talking to a small audience about their experiences of being beaten, shocked with cattle prods, thrown in jail, and spat on. I could hardly believe my ears. This was America? How could this be happening?

The Freedom Rides were the next high-profile protest event following the sit-ins in Greensboro, Nashville, and other southern cities. Actually the first Freedom Rides had taken place well in advance of the civil rights movement, in 1947. Bayard Rustin and George Houser, both members of CORE, had organized the "Journey of Reconciliation," a two-week tour of the South integrating buses on travel between states. They encountered lots of hostility, were arrested in North Carolina, and spent almost a month on a chain gang.

The idea was resurrected in 1961 by James Farmer, head of CORE. Members of CORE were joined by people from SNCC, the civil rights group formed after the Greensboro sit-ins. The idea was to take advantage of the 1960 U.S. Supreme Court ruling that had overturned laws segregating interstate travel (*Boynton v. Virginia*). The first Freedom Ride started in Washington on May 4, 1961, and was to arrive in New Orleans two weeks later. Some thirteen riders—seven black and six white—boarded Greyhound and Trailways buses and sat throughout the coach as they traveled through Virginia and North Carolina into South Carolina, Alabama, Mississippi, and Louisiana. The first incidents occurred in Charlotte, twenty miles south of Davidson, where several arrests were made, and Rock Hill, a small town in South Carolina near Charlotte, where John Lewis was beaten. Charles Sherrod was part of that demonstration. These events were nothing compared to what would happen next. In Birmingham, police stood by while a white mob attacked the riders, and in Anniston, Alabama, whites attempted to blow up the bus with the riders inside, setting the bus on fire. When the second bus arrived hours later, Klansmen entered it and beat the civil rights workers with pipes, bicycle chains, and baseball bats. The riders were forced to abandon their journey, but part of their mission had been accomplished because the events made their way onto the front pages of the nation's newspapers. The Kennedy administration was forced to get involved and plead for restraint by both sides.

Numerous Freedom Rides occurred after that. Diane Nash, one of the leaders in the Nashville sit-ins—and, in the spring of 1961, a leader in SNCC—organized the second bus trip from Nashville to Birmingham, where the activists were arrested and jailed. There was considerable violence experienced on most of the rides; and responding to calls for help, many supporters came down from the North. When the first Freedom Ride continued on to Montgomery, a rally was held in Ralph Abernathy's church, where more than fifteen hundred people heard Martin Luther King Jr. speak. In all, more than sixty Freedom Rides occurred in 1961 with more than 450 people participating, most ending up in jail and many beaten severely. In the fall of 1961 President Kennedy issued an executive order telling the Interstate Commerce Commission to start enforcing the laws desegregating interstate travel. Jim Crow signs on drinking fountains and the doors of restrooms started coming down in bus stations all over the South.

I do not know which Freedom Ride the people who came to Davidson were participating in. Most of the Freedom Riders at the union that evening seemed barely older than college students themselves and most were white. Several talked about their Quaker affiliation and said they were doing this because of their faith. I walked back to the dorm shaking my head in admiration and disbelief.

Through Dr. G's provocative talks, meeting the Freedom Riders, and seeing events unfold across the South, I slowly began to notice that racial segregation and injustice were a part of life at Davidson, although at the time my friends and I did not think of it as strange. The school had always been segregated. My future father-in-law, Grier Martin, was president of the college at the time. Raised in the South but enlightened for his era, he recognized that change was on the horizon and that Davidson would soon admit black students. Through his leadership, during my junior year the trustees voted to admit two students from Africa.

Even this measure was considered radical and controversial. I was stunned by the reactions of some of my fellow students from the Deep South. In Nashville I had never heard such venom as came out of their mouths. And most of these Davidson students were not uneducated, poor, white, working-class malcontents. They were from middle- and upper-class families.

★★★

Still, the earthshaking events that the Freedom Riders were experiencing seemed far away to me, almost as if they were happening in another country. The real turning point came in the summer of 1963, before my senior year, working in the Lower East Side of Manhattan.

I applied to work on the Lower East Side in one of the mission churches owned by Trinity Episcopal Church on Wall Street. Trinity owned two mission churches—or "chapels" as they were called—on

Henry Street. One of the chapels, St. Christopher's, was located almost under the Brooklyn Bridge; the other, St. Augustine's, was about a mile away. The program involved my living on the residential floor at St. Christopher's and walking down Henry Street, with its teeming tenements and vast public housing projects, to St. Augustine's to lead vacation Bible school. About a dozen college students were involved in the program, all white except for one young woman.

I had never been to New York and really had no idea what to expect. I rode up from Nashville with two high school friends who were headed to New England to work in summer camps. They dumped me at the first spot they could find after emerging from the Holland Tunnel into Manhattan. Even though it was still early June, the city was sweltering and shrouded in smog. I managed to flag down a cab, which took me along jammed, narrow streets with towering office buildings, then through Little Italy and Chinatown, where I thought I had suddenly landed in a different country. I could feel a surge of energy and excitement—this was the New York I had imagined, the Promised Land.

Before the program started we were given a reading list. Two books—*The Suburban Captivity of the Churches* by Gibson Winter and *Light the Dark Streets* by C. Kilmer Myers—particularly inspired me and helped form my consciousness about the social problems of the city and how to address them. The Winter book argued that starting in the 1950s churches had turned their backs on the social problems our country was facing by fleeing to the suburbs and closing down inner-city churches. That rang very true to me. It was the Myers book, however, that opened up a new way of looking at the mission of the church and how Christianity could be relevant. C. Kilmer Myers painted a grim picture of a Henry Street neighborhood plagued by racial discrimination, poor schools, broken families, gangs, drugs, crime and violence, and the need for God's redemptive love. As he became involved in the life of the community, people became involved in church activities and focused on community organization and problem solving. In his view this was what doing God's will was all about.

Many things that happened that summer changed my life. Most important, I was able to establish good friendships with people very different from me. Ed ("Bucky") Corey was an African American who grew up in the projects in New York and had received a scholarship to a New England prep school, where he was a rising junior. Ed was tall, fit, good-looking, and sophisticated with a slight touch of cynicism. He already looked and talked like an Ivy Leaguer. I felt very close to him throughout the summer.

Another friend was Rubio. Rubio was a blond Puerto Rican (hence his name, which means blond) and the polar opposite of Ed. He was short and scruffy. Also of high school age, he had dropped out of school and his English was marginal. Rubio's claim to fame was that he was vice president of the Bopping Ballerinas, one of the Puerto Rican street gangs in the area, and was the father of three kids—all with different mothers. Everyone knew Rubio. When we walked down the street, he would attract crowds of young followers like the Pied Piper. The thing about Rubio that impressed me most was that he never met a door he could not unlock. This came in very handy a couple of times when we were locked out of the church.

Rubio was working for the church that summer thanks to a pilot project funded by the Ford Foundation called the Gray Areas Program and later renamed Mobilization for Youth. The initiative was one of the first in the nation to try to bring disenfranchised and alienated young people into the mainstream with jobs, activities, and a focus on community building. At least for the summer of 1963 it seemed to be working, as Rubio helped organize games and competition and helped me keep some of the tougher kids in my vacation Bible school class in line.

Even though gang violence persisted and the living conditions were crowded and bleak, there was optimism about what was happening in New York and the Lower East Side. Much of this optimism came from the Gray Areas/Mobilization for Youth activities and the commitment of human and financial resources by church groups like Trinity Parish, social organizations like the Henry Street Settlement House, and the city. Part of the agenda in the Lower East Side Mission was civil rights. Almost every day someone from the church was picketing a construction site where contractors discriminated against minorities, and I was often on the picket line. I had never done anything like this before, but it seemed right as I carried a poster and chanted along with everyone else. There were other issues like the city government's hiring practices favoring whites.

A lot of conversation around dinner centered on what was going on in the civil rights movement on the new battlefields in the hard-core states—Mississippi, Alabama, and Georgia. Another frequent topic of discussion was the March on Washington for Jobs and Freedom, which was being planned for the end of the summer.

As during my home confinement with polio and my time in Mexico, the clergy had a great impact on me. What I saw on Henry Street brought me a sense of optimism about the role of the church in bringing about social change. There were several full-time priests divided between the two chapels. For the most part they were sharp, sophisticated, self-confident, and committed to their work. They had a good sense of humor and loved what they were doing. They saw their efforts as part of a much larger movement for profound social change. They believed that a major cause of inequality and poverty was the way society worked—institutional racism, voter disenfranchisement, and discriminatory business practices. To really help people you had to change the laws and the rules of the game. Providing meals at soup kitchens or handing out used clothes were fine as far as they went, but what was really needed was what they called "systemic change." They saw this as part of their Christian calling.

It all made a lot of sense to me. For a very long time I had been aware that America was far from being a land of equality, but this was when I began to understand why this was the case and what had to be done to change it. After my New York experience, I was a different person from who I was when I arrived in New York. At the end of the summer I was pumped up, excited, and ready to go back to college and make a difference during my senior year.

Chapter Seven:

The Movement Picks Up Steam

B y the summer of 1963, when I was winding up my work in the Lower East Side, the civil rights movement had come a long way from the sit-ins and the Freedom Rides of the early 1960s. Many injustices had come under attack. One was the voter registration process. In the Deep South it was not unusual for blacks who tried to vote to be assessed heavy poll taxes and forced to take "literacy tests," which often involved answering obscure questions and reciting the Constitution verbatim. In Mississippi a civil rights organization called the Regional Council of Negro Leadership had been around since the 1950s. Three of its leaders—Amzie Moore, Medgar Evers, and Aaron Henry—asked SNCC in 1961 to help register voters and organize the black community. A New York high school teacher named Bob Moses joined SNCC about that time and took the lead in organizing what became known as the Mississippi Project. In the fall of 1961, about the same time that the Freedom Riders came to Davidson, he started the first voter registration effort in McComb, Mississippi. The white response was immediate, resulting in numerous beatings and arrests.

Moses concluded that the efforts of all the civil rights groups would be needed, and in February 1962, SNCC, the NAACP, and CORE formed the Council of Federated Organizations (COFO). When later that year SCLC joined as well, the civil rights movement in Mississippi became a concerted effort. The beatings and arrests continued but so did the registration efforts, which focused on various Mississippi Delta counties and towns—Greenwood, Hattiesburg, Laurel, and

Holly Springs—and spread to Alabama, Georgia, Louisiana, and South Carolina.

A second major event in 1962 was James Meredith's attempt to enroll at the University of Mississippi. Governor Ross Barnett, supported by state police, blocked his entry to the campus, resulting in white rioting and two fatalities. Eventually the Kennedy administration had to call in U.S. marshals and the U.S. Army to enforce the law.

The third major event of 1961–62 was the Albany movement. This was another high-profile effort involving SNCC, the NAACP, and SCLC. The movement began in the fall of 1961 when Charles Sherrod, Cordell Reagon, and Charles Jones—all from SNCC—started a grassroots campaign to desegregate Albany, Georgia. The local leader was William Anderson, a physician. The difference between the Albany initiative and the sit-ins and Freedom Rides was that in Albany, the effort focused on all aspects of segregation—lunch counters, buses, libraries, swimming pools, voter registration, and schools. The idea was ambitious, and the organizational effort was the most impressive to date, with thousands of people participating in mass meetings, sit-ins, demonstrations, and boycotts. To keep the momentum going, SNCC invited SCLC and Martin Luther King Jr. to get involved. King came to Albany in December 1961, about a month after the demonstrations began. There was already some friction between SCLC and SNCC, since some in SNCC felt that during the Freedom Rides SCLC had left the heavy lifting to SNCC and CORE. This was SCLC's opportunity to step up to the plate and it did, putting all its prestige and King's behind the effort. King was arrested along with the SNCC leaders and several hundred other demonstrators during his first visit in December. He was locked up after declining bail. In July he was arrested again, along with Ralph Abernathy. This time the bail was paid anonymously, and King and Abernathy were forced to leave the jail.

There is some controversy as to whether the Albany movement was a success or failure. It was initially judged a failure by SCLC, which called off the effort in the fall of 1962 almost a year after it began, with no substantive concessions having been granted by the city. SCLC called it a learning experience and vowed to use different tactics, which it did in Birmingham and Selma, where the movement would focus on more specific targets. However, the Albany effort was successful in other ways. Through grassroots organizing led by SNCC, the Albany movement mobilized a high percentage of the town's black community. The organizational tactics—mass meetings, demonstrations, and grassroots mobilization of church members—were later used on other battlegrounds.

And SNCC stayed on. The movement gradually spread to other places in southwest Georgia. In the town of Moultrie and in Mitchell, Lee, and Baker Counties, efforts were made to organize the black community, desegregate public facilities and schools, and register voters. Voter registration efforts in Albany were particularly successful, resulting in one black candidate getting enough votes to force a runoff election for city council only months after King and SCLC departed. The Albany movement produced a new group of leaders, including Sherrod, Reagon, and Jones. It also produced the SNCC Freedom Singers, led by Reagon and his future wife, Bernice Johnson, who went on to found the legendary a capella group Sweet Honey in the Rock.

What diminished the effectiveness of the Albany movement were the actions of Police Chief Laurie Pritchett. Pritchett had studied the civil rights tactics used in other cities. He was determined not to give the demonstrators any opportunity to bring Albany adverse national publicity, so he directed the police to avoid violence. He also dispersed the more than one thousand people arrested to jails all over southwest Georgia, thus reducing photo opportunities for the press and television. It seemed to work, since Albany never got the national attention of other civil rights battlegrounds, and the Albany movement gradually lost steam. What was happening in Albany was quite distant from my world at Davidson, though from watching the evening news I was vaguely aware that civil rights activity was going on there. I never would have guessed that four years later—in the summer of 1966—I would find myself stumbling into the SNCC office in Albany after an all-night ride from New York City with several classmates from divinity school and with my bride of six months.

By 1962, civil rights demonstrations, boycotts, protests, and mass meetings were happening all over the South, many in small towns and rural counties in the Deep South. SNCC provided the foot soldiers for much of this effort, which rarely received national attention but was important in bringing about change from the bottom up. SCLC, however, was focusing on higher profile targets with the potential for national exposure. It next targeted Birmingham, which was important for a number of reasons. Birmingham was one of the most segregated cities in the South and one of the most oppressive for blacks. There black incomes were less than half of white incomes, black unemployment was high, and black voter registration was only 10 percent. The local government had the reputation of being brutal and uncompromising. There were so many unsolved bombing cases involving black homes and businesses between 1945 and 1962 that the city earned the nickname "Bombingham." When a court ordered Birmingham to desegregate its public parks, the city closed them. Also, as one of the largest cities in the Deep South, it could attract national attention. If the nation could be shown how bad the system of segregation was in the South, this should help forge a national solution. The stakes were high. As it turned out, SCLC could not have chosen a better location.

The leader of the civil rights movement in Birmingham was Reverend Fred Shuttlesworth. When the city outlawed the NAACP in 1956, Shuttlesworth formed the Alabama Christian Movement for Human Rights, which pushed for desegregation. Shuttlesworth's church, Bethel Baptist, was bombed several times, as was his house. In 1962 he petitioned Birmingham Mayor Art Hanes to desegregate public facilities. The mayor responded by informing him that he had thrown the letter in the garbage. Shuttlesworth called King and asked for help, saying, "If you come to Birmingham, you will not only gain prestige, but really shake the country. If you win in Birmingham, as Birmingham goes, so goes the nation" (Hampton and Fayer, *Voices of Freedom*, 125).

King and SCLC agreed to help. Learning from what SCLC believed were tactical mistakes in Albany, they decided to focus on a few concrete requests and measurable solutions: the desegregation of Birmingham's downtown stores, fair hiring practices in shops and city employment, the reopening of public parks, and the creation of a biracial committee to oversee the desegregation of Birmingham's public schools.

Birmingham became according to many the seminal moment in the civil rights movement, paving the way for the national legislation introduced in 1963. The most important person in making this happen was Eugene Connor, known by everyone as "Bull." Bull Connor had established a reputation as a die-hard, hard-core segregationist with a mean spirit. He had served on the Birmingham city commission for several terms and run for the U.S. Senate twice and lost. In 1963 he had run for mayor in a bitter race and was defeated by a more moderate segregationist, Albert Boutwell, supported by the business establishment. Connor, who also lost his seat on the city commission in the election, refused to step down; and for a brief period, the city government was in turmoil. Finally Connor agreed to relinquish his seat and settled for the position of commissioner of public safety, which he had held before. The stage was set for a direct confrontation between SCLC and Connor.

SCLC started with a boycott of downtown stores, cutting retail sales by as much as 40 percent. This was just the beginning. SCLC leaders had their eyes set on Connor. They knew he was combative. They were pretty sure he would take the bait.

The plan for direct action was devised by Wyatt Tee Walker, a founding member of SCLC and its executive director. "My theory," Walker said, "was that if we mounted a strong nonviolent movement, the opposition would surely do something to attract the media, and in turn induce national sympathy and attention to the everyday segregated circumstance of a person living in the Deep South" (Bass, *Blessed Are the Peacemakers*, 96). His plan was called Project C, for "confrontation," and consisted of organizing marches and protests throughout the city against segregated public institutions. The protests began in April. Arrests followed, with several hundred protestors going to jail, and by April 10 Connor had an injunction requiring the protestors to stop. In Albany SCLC had honored such injunctions, hoping to get concessions from the city. In Birmingham it defied them. On Friday, April 12, King was arrested along with several hundred others, his thirteenth arrest. He was in jail for almost two weeks, during which time he wrote the famous "Letter from Birmingham Jail," responding to moderate white Alabama clergymen who had criticized him for using direct action, even though the action was nonviolent. King justified civil disobedience in Birmingham with the famous statement, "Injustice anywhere is a threat to justice everywhere."

The controversial part of Project C happened next. SCLC was running out of people willing to march or demonstrate, since so many were in jail and others were fearful of a violent response. James Bevel, SCLC's director of direct action, came up with the idea of enlisting schoolchildren to demonstrate. He pointed out that the sit-ins had started with students. This plan was called D-Day and later was known as "The Children's Crusade." Some people questioned the ethics of using children in possibly dangerous situations, but Bevel won the argument. On May 2, more than one thousand African American children of various ages skipped school, some of them jumping over walls to avoid locked gates. They assembled in a large downtown church and then headed to city hall for a direct confrontation. Bull Connor did not disappoint. More than twelve hundred people were arrested, half of them children, some as young as eight. The jails were now overflowing.

Connor now had a dilemma. There was no room for more prisoners. He could have followed Pritchett's strategy in Albany—disperse prisoners across the state—but for some reason he didn't. He brought in the police dogs and fire hoses. The first time those images of black children being bitten by dogs and leveled by fire hoses appeared on television around the nation and the world, the die was cast. How could anyone who was watching television in early May 1963 forget those pictures? I certainly couldn't. I still can't. Why can't we do something? I said to myself. How could any decent person stand by and allow this to happen? Others must have been asking themselves the same questions.

Soon Birmingham was a city under siege as the ranks of the marchers swelled. Clergy, celebrities, and ordinary people from all over the country joined the protestors. Kennedy ordered Army troops to restore order, as the whole world watched. Downtown business came to a halt. The business community pressured the elected officials to accede to SCLC's demands. Local officials held firm and refused. But by May 8 everyone had had enough, and King reported to the press that most of the demands had been met. Birmingham would desegregate lunch counters, restrooms, drinking fountains, and fitting rooms within ninety days, and stores would hire blacks as salesmen and clerks. Three days after the May agreement, however, a bomb destroyed the motel where King had been staying only hours before. More riots occurred—this time involving rock-throwing whites—again requiring U.S. Army troops to restore order. The house of King's brother, A. D. King, was bombed the same week. But changes were occurring. On May 21 the new mayor took office, and Connor was out of a job. In early June the Jim Crow signs started coming down.

Before my romance with Embry I dated a young woman from Birmingham. In early June 1963, just before my experience on the Lower East Side, I visited her family. The weekend trip got off to a bad start when her father, a businessman, asked me to join him in his library for what he described as a heart-to-heart talk. He poured himself a stiff drink of whisky, did not offer me anything to drink at all, sat down in his easy chair, did not offer me a seat, and got straight to the point.

"Young man," he said scowling, looking up at me, "all this stuff you have been reading about Birmingham is a bunch of lies made up by the Yankee press. It's these outsiders, rabble-rousers, and Communists that come down here and make our community look bad. We got along fine with our colored until these agitators showed up. Now look what they have done. They deserved to be thrown in jail, all of them, and should be run out of our city permanently."

I do not know why his comments shocked me. My girlfriend had warned me that her father was very conservative, but I was already changing my own attitudes, and I had been fortunate to have grown up in a tolerant and, by southern standards, progressive home. I was not prepared for being so physically close to someone who fit the stereotype of a southern racist. I kept my mouth shut; and when he had finished his short speech, he indicated that it was OK for me to leave. He had done his duty. I was thankful that he had not asked for a response.

The weekend concluded in one of the largest Methodist churches in Birmingham. The place was packed. We were seated near the front with my girlfriend's parents. The service was dull until the sermon, when the minister proclaimed that God had preordained segregation of the races and that outside agitators were doing the work of the devil. You could feel the energy surge from the congregation, which made the proceedings feel more like a football game than a church service. It was all I could do to keep from leaving. After the service hundreds of people stood in line to shake the preacher's hand.

My girlfriend was a sweet and kind person who did not share her parents' views on race. But my experience that weekend pretty much finished off our relationship.

The battle in Birmingham continued into the fall. In September the integration of Birmingham schools began. In mid-September a bomb destroyed the Sixteenth Street Baptist Church, killing four young girls. In Tuscaloosa, the governor of Alabama, George Wallace, defied the Kennedy administration by refusing to allow two black students to enter the University of Alabama, resulting in Kennedy's sending more troops to force Wallace and state troopers to step aside. The action spread to Mississippi, where that fall Medgar Evers, a civil rights activist working as field secretary for the NAACP, was murdered by the Ku Klux Klan.

Following Birmingham, King became a national figure—a hero to many—and the de facto head of the civil rights movement. He was poised to play a major role in the next chapter—the March on Washington—which was to follow at the end of the summer.

★★★

It was not the first time a march on Washington had been planned to protest segregation. In 1941 A. Philip Randolph, Bayard Rustin, and A. J. Muste sought to organize a march to protest discrimination against African Americans in war industries. All three men had been early advocates of desegregation and civil rights. They also had sampled socialist causes of one sort of another and had been union organizers. Muste, the only white person in the group, was an ordained minister in the Dutch Reformed Church and a pacifist. After President Roosevelt signed an executive order barring discrimination in the defense industry, the march was canceled.

In 1963 Randolph revived the idea and enlisted Rustin to help. All the major civil rights groups supported the planning—the NAACP, SCLC, SNCC, CORE, the National Urban League, and Randolph's group, the Brotherhood of Sleeping Car Porters. The organizers agreed on six goals: meaningful civil rights laws, a massive federal works program, full and fair employment, decent housing, the right to vote, and adequate, integrated education.

On Wednesday, August 28, more than two hundred thousand marchers walked peacefully from the Washington Monument to the Lincoln Memorial—a very high number in those days—about 80 percent African American. The heads of each civil rights group got speaking time—Roy Wilkins (NAACP), Martin Luther King (SCLC), John Lewis (SNCC), Whitney Young (Urban League), and A. Philip Randolph (Brotherhood of Sleeping Car Porters). Floyd McKissick (CORE) read James Farmer's speech since Farmer was in jail for demonstrating in Louisiana. Walter Reuther of the United Auto Workers also spoke, as did the singer Josephine Baker, the only female speaker. Musical performers included Mahalia Jackson; Bob Dylan; Peter, Paul, and Mary; Joan Baez; and Marian Anderson. The event got essentially full coverage on every major network. It was a national happening.

I sat in my parents' living room glued to the television set, taking in every speech and song and pining to be there. I could have been there.

Most of my fellow workers from Henry Street in New York made the trip. It was one of my decisions I regret most.

John Lewis's address blamed the Kennedy administration for inaction and complacency and was very critical of the government. The other speeches were not particularly memorable—except one, King's "I Have a Dream," which continues to be part of our national psyche. While in the end the march did not directly result in specific actions, indirectly it had an enormous impact by placing civil rights squarely on the national agenda and making the American public aware of the high stakes involved. In some respects it might have even been the high-water mark in the civil rights movement, giving it new energy and momentum and moving it very near the point of no return. Though many whites would continue to resist fiercely, there was no turning back now.

Chapter Eight:

Marching in Charlotte

In the fall of 1963 I headed back to Davidson for my senior year. In the short time since I enrolled, Davidson had at last begun to change. That fall James Farmer of CORE addressed the student body and you could hear a pin drop during his speech. It received more than polite applause, after which students filed out of the auditorium quietly. Even the hard-core segregationists knew that change was in the wind.

However, civil rights was not yet part of my personal agenda for my senior year at Davidson. Although I was following civil rights activities elsewhere with great interest, and was moved by what I saw, I did not see any obvious possibilities for civil rights activities at Davidson. This was something happening to *other* people and happening in *other* places, in places of extreme prejudice like Birmingham and Albany, Georgia, not North Carolina. The New York experience had done a lot to change that perception, but the Lower East Side of New York City was not the sleepy college town of Davidson. I was not yet ready to put myself on the line and fully join the civil rights movement, but I was beginning to toy with the idea.

Evidence of my ambivalence was an event which I shamefully admit I planned one lazy Saturday afternoon in early October when several of us in my fraternity were sitting around in the warm sun with nothing to do.

"I have an idea," I exclaimed. "Let's have a civil rights march."

My fraternity brothers were a bit puzzled.

I explained that I was not thinking about a *real* civil rights march. Those things happened in Washington and in the Deep South. My idea was to target the most obscure southern school we could find within reasonable distance of Davidson and to show up and picket a school event. We were just arrogant enough to think that we Davidson students were the sophisticated ones who knew what was going on but were not so committed that we would ever really join the movement. So it would be a spoof but a spoof on a serious subject. Just as many of us had been moved by James Farmer and by the March on Washington, we would challenge these other students in some backwoods school to put the civil rights question on their radar screen but in a fun sort of way.

After an initially skeptical response, my friends seemed to warm up to the idea. There were eight of us. We all believed in the civil rights cause ourselves, so we weren't hypocrites exactly. We just were not totally genuine. I explained that after getting our point across we could let the backwoods kids in on the joke and then maybe have a serious discussion. The model for this plan was our experience at Davidson with the Freedom Riders, who without much fanfare had showed up at the college union and gotten students to focus on civil rights issues. So we would be sort of like the Freedom Riders—just without the legitimate credentials.

The plan worked perfectly. After some initial research we concluded that our target was Montreat College, in the mountains of North Carolina near Asheville, about a two-hour drive from Davidson. One of our members' parents had a vacation house in Montreat, which could be used as a base. We did not know anything about the college except that it was a small, Presbyterian, co-ed liberal arts school in a very isolated area of the state. Doubtless students and faculty were not anywhere near as sophisticated or informed as us Davidson students. We spent the afternoon making posters and trying to borrow sleeping bags. By 5:00 p.m. we were headed for the mountains in two cars. The fall colors were spectacular, the sky perfectly blue, and the air warm yet crisp. The plan was to arrive in Montreat around 7:00, drop gear off at the vacation house and hit the college around 8:00 looking for any activity we could find. We would then set up a picket line and try to engage students in some kind of dialogue. The name of our group was LEAP, an acronym for "love, equality, and peace." Our slogan was "Integrate or disintegrate," which we prominently displayed on our posters. Though some of the members of our group were beginning to have some misgivings as we approached Montreat, I tried to keep up the morale and hold us together. I think some of our group thought I had completely lost it.

As luck would have it, not only was there activity on campus, there was a campus–wide dance. Bull's eye. We heard dance band music coming from a large building and parked some distance away. Stealthy as Green Berets, we peered in the windows and checked out the situation. The logical place for the picket line was in front of the main entrance to the large stone building. We hoisted our signs and started to march around in a large circle, chanting as loudly as we could, "Integrate or disintegrate!" with half of us shouting "integrate" and the other half shouting "or disintegrate." It did not take long for our voices to be heard; and within five minutes, the dance music had stopped, and a hundred very puzzled college students were staring at us in complete bewilderment.

Just as I was trying to figure out what to do next, I was saved by an earnest young faculty member who we later learned was a political science professor. He pushed his way through the crowd, saying, "It's OK, it's OK. It's LEAP, I know this group, it's OK."

"Who is the leader?" he demanded, and all fingers pointed at me. I detected some sheepish grins among our group. What was Howell going to do now? The young professor looked at me and said, "OK, we understand your cause and a lot of us agree with it. We are trying hard to make a difference here. We are not integrated yet, but it will happen. This is a small college and we are not in the mainstream."

This was too much for me. "Well, neither are we," I responded in an apologetic tone. "We are actually from Davidson, which is probably a lot like Montreat College; and we are not much farther along than you are. But we are trying, too." I am sure there must have been a lot of questions as to what we actually meant by "Integrate or disintegrate," but I also concluded that the Montreat students pretty much got it. They were mercifully forgiving, invited us to the dance, and the conversations continued as we got inside. We explained the Freedom Rider experience at Davidson and apologized for choosing to stage our little skit at their college. The music picked up, most of us danced a time or two, and by 11:00 we retreated to our base camp. There we took out our flashlights and hiked to the mountaintop, where we slept under the stars until sunrise. The orange sun rose above the fog in the valley, igniting the brilliant fall foliage. It was an experience most of us would remember for a long time.

But I remember it with mixed emotions. On the one hand, it could not have gone any better. We had pulled it off flawlessly according to our plan. We fooled them initially and ended up stimulating some thinking and reflection. On the other hand, we were frauds. We had trivialized the most important issue of our time. We were not really engaged ourselves. Segregation was someone else's problem. Intellectually we had it figured out; but in terms of commitment, we were not there yet. I realized that we were wrong and vowed that the next time we did anything like this it would be for real.

★★★

The age of innocence for my generation ended on November 22, 1963. As I was walking to class, there was a rush of activity, "The president's been shot. Kennedy has been shot," people were saying in panicked tones. I immediately turned around, skipped class, and headed to the college union, where the room with the TV was packed. Everyone was standing around, staring at the screen, not saying a word. Walter Cronkite was trying to explain a confusing situation. Suddenly someone handed him a piece of paper. Cronkite paused and began to read, "From Dallas, Texas, the flash, apparently official: President Kennedy died at 1:00 p.m. Central Standard Time, two o'clock Eastern Standard Time—some thirty-eight minutes ago . . ." As he said this, Cronkite removed his glasses and looked straight into the camera. His voice began to break and he put the glasses back on, apparently more to hide his eyes from viewers than to read. He said something about Vice President Johnson, but I didn't hear it, as two large guys who looked like football players joined hands and danced a jig, gleefully singing, "We did it, we did it!" They bolted out of the building, anxious to share the news with their friends. Someone said they were from Texas. Everyone else just stared in disbelief.

There is nothing good that can be said about this event, which shook the planet. Yet it is true that it set the stage for Lyndon Johnson to move forward on the civil rights legislation that Kennedy had proposed and whose fate in Congress was in some doubt. Some historians have conjectured that Kennedy would never have been able to get a significant civil rights law passed. Once the country began to come out of its shock and initial mourning, there was an apparent mandate to finish what Kennedy had started. A week after Kennedy's assassination, Johnson told a joint session of Congress that "no memorial oration or eulogy could more eloquently honor President Kennedy's memory than the earliest possible passage of the civil rights bill for which he fought so long." Johnson started with the legislation Kennedy had introduced in June 1963, which had been strengthened by the House Judiciary Committee. The bill was designed to make illegal all Jim Crow laws and discrimination against blacks by private businesses and to strengthen the government's ability to desegregate public schools. While the bill had the necessary votes in the House to pass, it was far from clear whether it would be possible to get a bill out of the Senate, where segregationists still controlled key committees and the filibuster had been used to stop all previous civil rights legislation.

The civil rights bill was the major focus of attention at the beginning of 1964. This was the backdrop when I received an invitation in the mail to attend a conference sponsored by students at Haverford and Bryn Mawr Colleges just outside Philadelphia. The conference title was "The Third Great American Revolution" (the American Revolution and the Civil War having been the first two), and representatives from all of the major civil rights groups were on the program. The event would be held at Bryn Mawr College toward the end of February, with overnight accommodations for men at Haverford. I decided to attend, and four other Davidson students joined me, none of whom I knew well. The attendance—several hundred people—exceeded all expectations, and most sessions were standing-room only. The speakers who made the greatest impression on me were James Farmer from CORE, James Forman from SNCC, and Dick Gregory, the famous black comedian, who was all seriousness at this event. Students came from across the country, but especially from the Northeast and the Mid-Atlantic. I do not recall any other southern schools being represented besides Davidson.

The speakers talked of their experiences in the civil rights movement—the sit-ins, Freedom Rides, voter registration efforts, and marches. I was generally aware that all these things were happening, but except for the Freedom Riders at Davidson I had never heard the gory details firsthand from people directly involved. It was hard not to be moved and impressed by their courage and determination. What came through were the speakers' pleas for help and direct involvement from conference attendees. Almost all the speakers were black, almost all the audience, white. Many of the participants were from Ivy League and other prestigious schools. Speaker after speaker said more or less the same thing: "White people of goodwill need to get involved and speak out, not sit on the sidelines. You are either for us or against us; and if you are for us, you have to jump into the fray. Get involved and make a difference. We need you." In three years this message would be replaced by something very different as Black Power became prominent; but for now, the civil rights movement needed white people. I was ready to sign up.

Driving back in the car on Sunday, at first nobody said very much. Then from the back seat a voice, that of a college freshman, said, "Well, what are *we* going to do about it?" This spurred a long, heated discussion that lasted from just outside of Philadelphia all the way to Davidson. When we rolled into Davidson late that evening, it was a done deal: We were going to organize a civil rights march in Charlotte in support of the civil rights bill. Toward the end of the ride I asked the logical question, "So who is going to lead the march?" The unanimous answer was, "Of course, you are." I had to admit that I was the obvious choice—I was the only senior in the car; and I was already a campus leader and a fraternity guy, not an independent as were most of the others. The fraternity system was pretty effective in casting independents as outside the mainstream. I paused for a moment and then said, "OK, let's go for it, but I am going to need your help organizing it." They all agreed and said they would take on the lion's share of the legwork.

The initial idea was to have a "Civil Rights March on Charlotte" just like the March on Washington the previous August. Then someone pointed out that Charlotte actually had a relatively good record on civil rights. In 1960 Charles Jones, later one of the leaders in the Albany movement, had organized more than two hundred people to protest segregated lunch counters in Charlotte and in Rock Hill, South Carolina; and Charlotte business leaders agreed to desegregate fairly quickly. No other incidents had gotten media attention, and race relations were described as generally good, though school integration in Charlotte did not start until the early 1970s. Charlotte's civic leadership was exclusively white but relatively progressive compared to that of most other southern cities. We agreed that the march would be "*in* Charlotte" not "*on* Charlotte."

The event that followed in the middle of March is not mentioned in the histories of the civil rights movement. This did not mean, however, that it was not significant for people directly touched by it—both those who participated and those who did not. It turned out to be a day of decision for Davidson students and faculty alike. Everyone had to decide where he stood on the issue and what kind of risk he was willing to take.

The plan was to enlist the support of students from the two major historically black colleges near Davidson—Barber Scotia College in Concord and Johnson C. Smith University in Charlotte. Both were founded by the Presbyterian Church in 1867, just after the Civil War, and both had impressive histories. Barber Scotia's mission was initially to provide education to "Negro women," primarily in the areas of teaching, social work, and homemaking, but it had since become co-ed; and Johnson C. Smith had a strong liberal arts program and an excellent theological school. We decided that the march would take place on Saturday, March 14, and that in advance we would circulate petitions in support of the civil rights bill. We would collect all the petitions and march about a mile from the campus of Johnson C. Smith to the downtown post office and mail them to President Johnson. There would be a rally beforehand at Johnson C. Smith with speeches and a party there following the march—all pretty innocuous compared to what was going on elsewhere in the country, especially in the Deep South. We had just under a month to pull the whole thing together.

The case we made for signing the petition was straightforward and identical for white and black audiences: segregation is wrong; the civil rights bill would go a long way toward righting that wrong; we support the bill. We found out who the student leaders were at Barber Scotia and Johnson C. Smith, met with them, and made presentations to larger groups. Everyone was very supportive, and we knew we could count on a good turnout from both schools. The Johnson C. Smith leaders were very helpful in getting the logistics lined up for use of their campus. We also made presentations at Queens College, a white all-women's school in Charlotte, where the response was tepid. There was really no way to know how well we would do with Davidson people. We held a number of informational sessions, wrote articles for the student newspaper explaining our position, and had a core group of fifteen to twenty dedicated workers who were fully committed and working hard on the logistics. I was both amazed and relieved that in the weeks leading up to the march, I got very little negative feedback from fellow students at Davidson. I knew that a lot of students—and some faculty members—profoundly disagreed with what we were doing. Several were in my fraternity. At the same time, I felt that we had their respect for standing up for what we thought was right.

Everything was not rosy, however. One of my good friends and an organizer and strong supporter of the march was Bill Ferris of Vicksburg, Mississippi. Both he and his parents received death threats in letters and postcards, forcing Bill to keep a low profile. Other students from the Deep South got similar letters. My parents received a postcard asking if they knew their son was "dancing with Nigger girls in the streets of Charlotte." My parents did know what was going on. Once the decision was made to charge ahead, I called them to give them a "heads up as to what your son has gotten himself into." After I explained to them what I was going to do and why, there was a long pause and then questions about my safety. If they disagreed with anything I was doing, they did not express this to me, and I got the general idea that they tacitly supported not only me but the cause.

Planning for the march was falling into place thanks to the help of the organizers, who as they had promised took care of all the logistics. On the Monday before the march was to take place I got a call from the president of Davidson, Grier Martin (my future father-in-law), to meet with him at his house around 7:00 p.m. I had been wondering when I would get this call. I was met by his wife, Louise, who graciously escorted me to the library where Grier rose and extended a hand, motioning me to sit down. He got straight to the point.

"Joe," he began in his slow southern drawl, "I've been following what you have been doing for some time and as you know have stayed on the sidelines; but now I must inform you that there is considerable pressure on me to ask you to call off the march." He went on to say that the mayor of Charlotte and the chairman of the Davidson College Board of Trustees had both contacted him and asked that he tell me to call it quits. They worried that the march would cause discord and worsen the generally good relationship between the races. They feared it would cast both Charlotte and Davidson College in a bad light. When I explained that the march was not *on* Charlotte but *in* Charlotte, and that it had nothing to do with Davidson College, Grier said that the mayor and trustees feared this distinction would be lost on most people.

But then he added, "Of course, you know that I can't *force* you to abandon the effort. I am doing my duty to convey these requests to you and to be sure you understand the seriousness of what you are up to." I thought I noticed a slight smile. I only later learned that Grier Martin had championed the cause of bringing African students to Davidson and had been working behind the scenes to fully integrate the college.

The other concern, he said, was the safety of the marchers. He asked me to call the mayor of Charlotte, Henry Belk, to discuss these concerns with him directly. As I left, he repeated his earlier comment that he could not force me to do anything. We shook hands and I departed smiling and very relieved.

I called Mayor Belk the next day. His voice rose immediately, and he practically ordered me to call off the march, though I stood my ground. If Grier Martin did not have the authority, I didn't think the mayor did either. He said he had only one concern—the safety of the marchers. "Do you know what a redneck is, son? Well, rednecks are uneducated whites who hate Negroes and who will stop at nothing to fight for segregation." He pointed out that our route would take us directly through a redneck neighborhood and that he could not guarantee our safety. If anything happened it would be our fault, and it would make Charlotte look bad, ruining what had been a very successful, moderate approach to the race issue. He repeated that to avoid potential disaster it would be best simply to call the whole thing off. After all, we had already gotten our point across. Since stories had been in the newspaper, conducting the march would serve no further purpose. I thanked him for his comments but made no concessions. After a long sigh, he hung up.

The day before the march, when we went through last-minute preparations, was an absolutely beautiful, early spring day—pale blue sky with puffs of white clouds and all shades of green in the budding trees. The day of the march, we woke up to overcast skies and a steady, cool rain. As the day progressed it rained harder and harder; and by the time the march got under way around 2:00 p.m., it felt like we were in a monsoon. I did not know whether there was any truth to the mayor's comments about hostile rednecks; but if there was, the rain was a godsend. The only people on the march route were police, reporters, and photographers, and there was no hint of the angry white mob the mayor feared.

Five hundred people marched that day—about 80 percent African American. We had about fifty college students from Davidson along with a half-dozen professors, as well as a number of white well-wishers from a Unitarian church in Charlotte. Everyone else was from Barber Scotia and Johnson C. Smith. Representatives from the schools all said a few words, and the keynote speech was given by an outspoken economics professor from Davidson, who said the only race he was a part of was "the human race." I talked about how for many of us this was the beginning, not the end, of the fight, and that the only real test as to whether the march was successful or not was whether we continued to be involved in supporting the cause in our own communities.

By all accounts, though modest in what we set out to achieve, the march was a huge success. Given the weather, we had a very good turnout. There was no violence. We got good TV and press coverage with lead stories on the local evening news and front-page articles in the *Charlotte Observer*. Perhaps best of all, black students and white students got to know each other and vowed to keep working together. And the party after the event was fun, with blacks and whites dancing together into the wee hours—a first experience for practically all of us white boys.

It turned out that getting the Civil Rights Act of 1964 passed was harder than we thought it would be when we planned the march. Southern senators used the filibuster to try to kill the legislation. After more than fifty days of debating, horse-trading, and filibustering, the bill's managers, Hubert Humphrey and Mike Mansfield, finally got sixty-seven votes, the first time the Senate had ever been able to overcome a civil rights filibuster. Helping the cause was the national coverage of the demonstrations in St. Augustine, Florida, in the spring, where King was arrested and thrown in jail again along with the seventy-two-year-old mother of the governor of Massachusetts. There were wade-ins, brutal beatings, and more images of police brutality (now becoming routine on national television), all of which put pressure on wavering senators. On July 2, 1964, President Johnson signed the Civil Rights Act into law.

I would like to think our march played a small role in moving the bill forward, but of course it didn't. But it did do a lot of other things. It raised the level of consciousness about civil rights for a lot of people on the Davidson campus and in the surrounding area. It forced many people to face the issue head on and decide where they stood, and it gave many people the opportunity to stand up for an important cause. And, perhaps most important, while a relatively minor event, it was one of many actions in support of civil rights that were beginning to happen in communities around the country. Collectively they were beginning to make a difference.

It turned out that the hardest part for me was dealing with the notoriety in the days and weeks that followed. There were numerous letters to the editor of the *Charlotte Observer*, most of them critical, and I received close to a hundred letters myself, about 90 percent of them critical and some outright hostile. It wasn't the tone of the letters that bothered me, it was the anxiety associated with suddenly being thrust into the spotlight and feeling unprepared for it. I had no trouble with this before the march but had not bargained for the aftermath.

The day after the march, the conservative *Nashville Banner* picked up the story from the *Charlotte Observer* and ran a front-page article with the headline "Banker's Son Leads Rights March." The article began, "Joseph Toy Howell III, son of Nashville banker Joseph Toy Howell Jr...."

A lot of people have asked me about my parents and how they dealt with my notoriety within the Belle Meade establishment. If they suffered, they never told me about it. My parents were so entrenched in Nashville society, such pillars of the community, and generally so loved and respected, there was not much people could do to dislodge them. When I asked them years later what it had been like in those days, my mother replied that they were treated by some friends—but not all that many—as if their son had flunked out of college, gotten into drugs, gotten into trouble with the police, or declared himself a member of the Communist Party. The most common reaction was that my parents should not take it personally, that they were good parents who had done all they could to raise their son correctly; but despite all one's best efforts, awful things like this sometimes happened. The most likely venues for such comments were the regular cocktail parties after everyone had had a couple of drinks. My mother said her typical response was to thank the people for their sympathy. She would smile, then look them squarely in the eye and say casually that actually she was quite proud of her son. That usually ended the conversation. Before long people stopped bringing up the issue.

But not everyone did. When I returned to Nashville after my senior year, I went over to the house of one of my best friends and had the door slammed in my face by his mother, who had always been one of my favorite people among the parents of my friends. She wagged her finger at me as if to say shame, shame, and warned me never to set foot in their yard again. "You are a disgrace and are not welcome in our house or in this city." I got similar but much less severe treatment from a few other people, mainly in my parents' generation. Most of my Nashville friends acted as if nothing had ever happened.

The other aspect of the aftermath that I had not anticipated was the beginning of my friendship with Al Lowenstein. I had never heard of Al Lowenstein before the spring of 1964. At 8:00 a.m. on the Monday after the march, as my roommate and I were trying to sleep in, there was a knock on our dorm room door. It was a postman with a special delivery letter for me. I had no idea how he had found me in the dorm and was stunned that someone would send me a special delivery letter—especially one delivered at such an early hour. This was the first of perhaps a half-dozen special delivery letters over the next several weeks. I opened the envelope and found a crumbled piece of paper with an American history test on one side. (I was an American history major and found the essay questions very difficult.) On the other was a hand-scribbled, barely legible note saying, "Saw you on TV. Call me at noon at this telephone number." It was signed "Al." I figured his last name was Lowenstein because that was the name of the professor who had given the test. The class was at North Carolina State University.

I was free at noon, so I found a pay phone and called the number. The person at the other end answered simply, "Al." This was the beginning of a relationship that would last some fifteen years until Al Lowenstein's assassination in March 1980. Al befriended a whole lot of young people, and I was just one in a throng of groupies, but his dynamic and somewhat eccentric personality inspired and motivated many in my generation, not only in the area of civil rights but in the peace movement and various social justice and progressive causes.

Allard Lowenstein was in many ways a quintessential New Yorker. His father was a successful restaurant owner in Manhattan, and the family had a spacious apartment on the Upper West Side. He attended the prestigious Horace Mann School for high school; but instead of going on to one of the Ivy League colleges, he chose the University of North Carolina at Chapel Hill, where he became active in student government. In his senior year, 1950, he was elected president of the National Student Association. He was a protégé of UNC's progressive president, Frank Porter Graham (also briefly a U.S. senator), and became passionately interested in various progressive causes. He earned a law degree from Yale and served two years in the U.S. Army. In 1959 Al wrote one of the first exposés of apartheid in South Africa in a book called *Brutal Mandate.*

To this day Lowenstein remains a controversial and in some ways enigmatic figure. One of his biographers asserts that he was secretly working for the CIA most of the time he was involved in progressive causes. He ran for the U.S. Congress several times and the Senate twice and served one term as a Democratic U.S. congressman from Long Island. He organized the Dump Johnson Campaign, which resulted in Johnson's dropping out of the 1968 presidential race. He was assassinated in 1980 at age fifty-one by a former Stanford student who was mentally ill. But all this does not begin to describe Al Lowenstein. One of the biographies of Lowenstein is *The Pied Piper,* and this is an apt title. He had an uncanny way of inspiring and motivating idealistic young people, and I was one of his easy converts.

My first conversation with Al led to his meeting me at a coffee shop on Main Street in Davidson. He was on his way to a meeting in Charlotte. He was almost an hour late, one of his trademarks, and half-heartedly apologized. He was about medium height, had a very short crew cut, large biceps, a big chest that made him look like a wrestler (which he was in college), and wore thick horned-rimmed glasses. He looked much younger than his thirty-five years. He was somewhat disheveled—he would always look disheveled—and was carrying a stack of papers, giving him the appearance of an absent-minded professor. We shook hands. He had a warm smile, though I was aware that he did not look me in the eye. This was another one of his idiosyncrasies. He rarely looked people in the eye—at least not for very long. He talked very fast and got right to the point. He was involved in organizing what he called "COFO Summer" in Mississippi and wanted to know if he could count on me to join him in the effort to register voters in Mississippi.

During that conversation and many subsequent conversations that would follow, I learned that he seemed to know just about everyone in the country involved in progressive causes and seemed to wind up at the center of the action. He had been a protégé of Eleanor Roosevelt. He seemed to know all the civil rights leaders and most of the liberal congressmen and senators. He had an uncanny ability to show how events were connected and give the impression he had inside information as to what was really going on. He was an unapologetic champion of liberalism—of using the power of government to address wrongs and make the world a better place. Civil rights was his cause of the day. He was a true evangelist. He also had a wry sense of humor. I thought he was just about the smartest and most articulate person I had ever met.

I was not able to go to Mississippi with him that summer; but he and one of his friends, Ed King, a white Methodist minister from Mississippi who was a veteran of many civil rights battles—and whose face was disfigured by the Klan—visited me at my parents' home in Nashville at the end of the summer of 1964. They stayed there overnight as they were headed from Mississippi to Washington in an effort to promote the Mississippi Freedom Democratic Party. My parents listened attentively as Al and Ed described the many beatings and various confrontations they had witnessed. My parents were aghast. I thanked my lucky stars I had an excuse for not participating in what Al had called COFO Summer. He and Ed talked about their strategy for getting delegates of the Mississippi Freedom Democratic Party—of which Ed was one— seated at the national Democratic Party convention to be held shortly in Atlantic City. I would stay in touch with Al for the next fifteen years and would continue to be inspired—and at times perplexed—by his magnetic personality.

The cause Al was trying to enlist me in was also called the "Mississippi Project" or "Freedom Summer," which was being led by Bob Moses of the Council of Federated Organizations. Moses was the head of COFO and came up with the idea of recruiting college students from all over the country to help with the major projects on COFO's agenda—voter registration, Freedom Schools, opening health and legal clinics, and the effort to form a new Democratic Party of African Americans that would challenge the established white Democratic Party. Moses had cut his teeth registering voters in McComb County; and though the numbers were not high, the effort showed that local blacks would respond and get involved. By bringing in college students, mainly from the North, the effort would be more likely to get the attention of the national media. SNCC leaders spent the spring making the pitch on college campuses. They recruited almost one thousand students, many from Ivy League and other prestigious schools like Stanford. The vast majority of them were white, and many were from affluent families—a demographic partly explained by the fact that participants were required to bring a minimum of five hundred dollars for bond money. Except for the fact that few if any were from the South, they were people a lot like me.

The goal of getting national publicity was achieved almost on day one. On June 21, 1964, three COFO workers were arrested for speeding and then mysteriously disappeared. James Cheney was a twenty-one-year-old black activist from Meridian. Michael Schwermer and Andrew Goodman, both white, were from New York City. Schwermer was a twenty-four-year-old CORE organizer and Goodman a twenty-year-old COFO volunteer and anthropology student. Schwermer and Goodman had arrived only the day before. Fearing the worst, President Johnson ordered an FBI investigation. The story got the attention of the national media. Despite the disappearance of their three colleagues, the COFO volunteers continued their work; and efforts to register voters as well as to set up alternative schools and health and legal clinics ultimately proved very successful. Two of our friends from New York worked in the Freedom Schools that summer and returned home with both war stories and optimism.

In 1964 fewer than 7 percent of the eligible black voters were registered. Though relatively few voters were registered that summer, the organization was put in place to make it happen; and following the Voting Rights Act of 1965, the effort mushroomed. By 1969 the portion of black Mississippians registered to vote reached almost 67 percent, 5 percent above the national average. Freedom Schools and health clinics started popping up across the state, and the Mississippi Freedom Democratic Party made a strong run at unseating the white delegation at the Democratic National Convention in Atlantic City.

While there were incidents of violence and lots of harassment, the rest of the volunteers returned at the end of the summer more or less intact. Many had battle scars for their efforts, and the statistics looked like those from a war: four civil rights workers killed (the fourth in a head-on collision), four people seriously wounded, eighty Freedom Summer volunteers beaten, more than one thousand people arrested (both volunteers and locals), and more than thirty churches bombed or burned, along with about the same number of black homes and businesses. And at the end of the summer before the volunteers returned home or to their colleges, the FBI found the bodies of Cheney, Schwermer, and Goodman—murdered apparently by the Ku Klux Klan.

Another bill that became law in 1964 would have a major impact on many African Americans and poor whites. This was the Economic Opportunity Act of 1964, which officially launched the federal "War on Poverty." The bill was signed into law on August 20, a month and a half after the Civil Rights Act. Modeled on ideas developed in the Ford Foundation's Mobilization for Youth Program, which I had witnessed while working on the Lower East Side, the bill's main focus was empowerment. Through it a number of programs were created, such as the Jobs Corps and Head Start, and funds were allocated for "community action programs" that would require poor people and African Americans to participate in the organizations that would oversee the use of War on Poverty dollars. When Embry and I found ourselves in southwest Georgia in 1966, Head Start and the community action programs were just getting under way.

The summer of 1964 therefore marked a turning point for me in many ways. I now had a college degree and was ready for the next phase of my life. What I did not know was that my involvement in the civil rights movement was far from over.

Chapter Nine:

Off to New York City

The year 1964 was big for me in more ways than getting involved in civil rights. In the spring of that year, one of my friends arranged for me to have a date with Embry Martin, a freshman at Randolph-Macon Women's College in Lynchburg, Virginia. I had met her once before but did not really know her. I also was a bit wary because she was the daughter of Grier Martin, the president of the college, and I was a controversial figure on campus by then. That first date—which occurred several weeks after the Charlotte civil rights march—was the beginning of a romance that led to our marriage in December 1965. Embry was unlike anyone I had ever met before—very intelligent, inquisitive, thoughtful, and quite secure in who she was. She had a freshness and a great sense of adventure about her that were rare; and, probably most important, we shared the same values. From the summer of 1964 on, she was at the center of my life and was involved in just about everything I was involved in. The journey of one along the path of the most important social issue of our time became the journey of two.

In the fall of that year, I was headed off to New York to attend Union Theological Seminary. While I was energized and inspired by the role of the clergy in the Lower East Side, I still I wasn't sure of my calling to the ministry. I wasn't sure that my faith was strong enough. I had become a questioner, a borderline agnostic, which made it hard for me to go along with the Christian program. I applied for a Rockefeller Fellowship, designed for college seniors who did not know what they wanted to do with their lives but who were leaders in college. The fellowship provided all expenses for a year of seminary to test it out and see if the ministry might be right for them. If it stuck, perhaps the church would pick up someone with talent who otherwise might have ended up as a lawyer or businessperson. If it [The referent is "the church," and in my editing I otherwise treated institutions as singular entities with singular pronouns.] didn't, maybe they would get a more informed layperson.

I received the fellowship and chose Union Seminary in New York for several reasons. First, it was in New York City, and I loved New York. Second, it was nondenominational, which I thought—probably wrongly it turned out—would give me a better perspective on the ministry. Third, Union was considered by many to be the preeminent theological school in the country, if not the world, having had the likes of Paul Tillich and Reinhold Niebuhr on its faculty and Dietrich Bonhoeffer as one of its students. Located on the Upper West Side, Union provided opportunities to take classes at Columbia, which was only a block away. But most important for me was Union's history as a center for progressive Christian thought and social activism. It seemed to be out front in taking courageous stands on controversial social issues and was clearly committed to the civil rights cause.

I arrived at Union on a hot, sticky day in late August 1964. I was happy to be there and to study at such a famous institution. Unfortunately my sense of wonder and excitement did not last very long. I soon discovered that many of my classmates were just like me—student leaders in college, progressive, committed to social justice and civil rights, achievers, and absolutely clueless as to what they wanted to be when they grew up. I think Union would have been perfect for someone really grounded and committed to a career in the ministry or a related field—and there were a few of those. But, having arrived already with doubts about my vocation, Union's lack of structure or religious discipline caused me to feel adrift. I remember occasionally trying to get through some complicated reading and staring out the window at the people walking past and the children playing across the street and concluding that I had somehow ended up in prison.

It was a sign of the times. The country was in the midst of one of the most important social revolutions in its history, and here we were in a classroom trying to understand an obscure passage in Genesis or the "Christology" of the New Testament. People were putting their lives on the line in Mississippi and Alabama. They were just starting to protest the Vietnam War. I was not alone; of those who graduated in my class, fewer than 20 percent went on to be ordained or to work in a job directly related to a church, an all-time low for Union.

★★★

During my first year at Union my most important experience was my fieldwork at St. Mark's-in-the-Bowery, a historic Episcopal church on the Lower East Side in the East Village. Part of the experience involved being assigned to a family who would invite me to dinner, help me get acclimated in the church community, and become a kind of home away from home. The husband was named Hector. He was born in Puerto Rico and had been a teenage gang member on the Lower East Side before he became involved in the work of Trinity Parish, joining St. Augustine's, the same church I had worked at in 1963. That is where he met Mary, a white college graduate from a middle-class New Jersey family, who was a church worker just like I had been. They fell in love, got married, and had produced five stair-step children ages three to twelve. They lived in one of the large public-housing projects not far from the church. Hector worked in the garment district, where he hauled clothes from one business to another, and Mary stayed home with the kids. They both were in their mid-thirties. I had dinner with them on Thursday evenings following my fieldwork, and they made me feel like one of the family.

For me their marriage was living proof that the lines of class, race, and ethnicity could be overcome. They were warm and loving and represented in my mind some kind of Holy Grail, a sign that our human differences could be transcended and that there truly was a happily ever after.

The idyllic view slowly began to crack. On Saturday mornings I accompanied Hector to basketball games where he coached a rough group of teenagers playing on the St. Mark's Church team. It soon became obvious that most of the time Hector showed up reeking of alcohol, sometimes so drunk he could not walk straight. I tried not to think too much about it, though it was shocking to me that at 9:00 in the morning he was in such bad shape. Then there were signs that everything was not going so well at home. Toward the end of my second year with them, Mary did not seem to be her usual happy and loving self. I began to feel tension in the home. One afternoon I showed up unannounced and was stunned by what I saw. Mary's face was swollen and black and blue with bruises, and she had bruises all over her arms. She looked like she should be in the hospital. When I naively asked her what had happened, she looked at the floor and sheepishly said she had fallen in the bathtub. It did not seem all that plausible, but I accepted what she said.

Two weeks later when I had my monthly meeting with the rector of the church, he casually told me that Mary had left Hector and taken all the kids with her and was in a secret location. I was flabbergasted. My ideal world had just fallen apart. The rector, a sophisticated, somewhat cynical person, asked how I could be so naive as to miss the signs or to think that a marriage between a former Puerto Rican gang member, who could hardly speak English, and a white, middle-class college graduate could ever last in the first place.

"What did you expect, Joe?" he asked sarcastically. "Grow up."

The image of Mary with her distorted face and of Hector staggering to Saturday basketball games is as strong now as it was then. I wonder what kind of suffering they must have gone through and wonder whatever happened to all of them. Someone told me years later that Mary had become a nun.

Did this mean that there was no way that deep cultural differences could be overcome? Did it mean that I was naive to think blacks and whites and Hispanics could transcend the barriers of race and class? Did it mean that someday I would become calloused and cynical like the priest of St. Mark's? Did it mean that the Holy Grail of overcoming these barriers was a hopeless illusion? All these questions haunted me in my second year at Union Seminary.

★★★

In the fall of 1964 and spring of 1965, while we Union students were sitting on the sidelines, the civil rights movement was having one of its busiest and most important years. Martin Luther King Jr. had been awarded the Nobel Peace Prize in December 1964, giving more credibility to the movement and prestige to its leaders. SNCC was doing grassroots organizing throughout the Deep South. Malcolm X was assassinated in Harlem only blocks from Union Seminary. Battles seemed to be happening everywhere.

One of the places the movement was having the most difficulty in was Selma, Alabama. Like Bull Connor, the sheriff of Selma, Jim Clark, was known for his brutality and belligerence. Local residents turned to SCLC. The stage was set for a Birmingham-type confrontation with the potential for a great deal of media coverage. SCLC named James Bevel head of the Selma movement. King came down and participated in several marches and was arrested along with about 250 other demonstrators. In February 1965, during the second semester of my first year at Union, Jimmie Lee Johnson, a civil rights worker from the neighboring town of Marion, was shot and killed by a state trooper in a peaceful demonstration. This prompted Bevel to up the ante in Selma. He came up with a plan that involved marching fifty-four miles from Selma to Montgomery, the state capital. Hosea Williams of SCLC and John Lewis of SNCC agreed to lead some six hundred demonstrators. On March 7, 1965, only minutes into the march, when approaching the now infamous Edmund Pettus Bridge, the marchers were stopped by state troopers, many on horseback and wielding tear gas, chains, barbed wire, billy clubs, and bull whips. Sixteen marchers were hospitalized, and John Lewis was knocked unconscious. As in Birmingham, journalists were there to film and photograph the mayhem, which was the lead story on network newscasts and on the front pages of major newspapers. Two days later, when some marchers returned to the scene, someone in a white mob shot and killed the Reverend James Reeb, a white, thirty-eight-year-old Unitarian minister from Boston. The Selma incident prompted President Johnson to address a joint session of Congress the next week and plead for passage of what became Voting Rights Act of 1965, using the language of the civil rights movement:

> But even if we pass this bill, the battle will not be over. What happened in Selma is part of a far larger movement which reaches into every section and state of America. It is the effort of American Negroes to secure for themselves the full blessings of American life. Their cause must be our cause, too. Because it's not just Negroes, but really it's all of us, who must overcome the crippling legacy of bigotry and injustice. And we shall overcome.

When two weeks later the march resumed, there were over eight thousand marchers, many having come to Selma from great distances. Most of the marchers were black, but there were many whites, including a number of celebrities. The rector of my fieldwork church, St. Mark's, was one of the marchers. Because of a deal worked out with the authorities, only three hundred demonstrators were allowed to make the whole march, but the images on television of the throngs crossing the bridge were stunning. The marchers reached Montgomery five days later, March 25, without incident. There they staged a huge rally called "Stars for Freedom." Performers included Harry Belafonte; Tony Bennett; Frankie Laine; Peter, Paul, and Mary; Sammy Davis Jr.; and

Nina Simone. The next day some twenty-five thousand people marched from the Catholic Church to the capitol. That evening Viola Liuzzo, a white mother of five, was assassinated by the Ku Klux Klan while she was driving participants back to Selma.

Many historians have said that Selma was a major influence in the passage of the Voting Rights Act of 1965, which Johnson signed into law on August 6. This law created the framework allowing massive voter registration in the South. Within four years the number of African Americans registered to vote in the Deep South had more than doubled, and blacks were being elected to office. In 1965, when the law was enacted, there were only about one hundred black elected officials in the entire country, almost all in the North. By 1989 some seventy-two hundred African Americans held elected office, more than forty-eight hundred in the South. A revolution had happened. By the beginning of the twenty-first century the number was well over nine thousand black elected officials nationwide, with a solid majority of them in southern states.

★★★

My courtship with Embry Martin continued during my first year at Union, and the intense relationship was not easy since we saw little of each other. She took the bus to New York several times, and twice we met in Washington, which was halfway—but still it was a long-distance romance. It was the next summer, the summer of 1965, before we really had much time to spend together. I got a summer fieldwork position in Boston City Hospital, Boston's massive inner-city, public hospital, as a chaplain in what was called a "clinical training program" for prospective clergy; Embry was working as a counselor in a church-sponsored summer camp for kids from lower-income families in Roxbury, Boston's largest black ghetto. She lived near her camp, and I stayed with other seminary students in a dorm of a theological school in Newton Center. We went to concerts at the Boston Pops, traveled one weekend to Tanglewood, the summer home of the Boston Symphony, and to Cape Cod on another, and spent lots of time strolling through Boston Common and the Public Garden and getting to know the city and each other.

Work was hard and challenging for both of us. Embry's job involved working with low-income black kids in an underfunded and poorly managed church program. She was frustrated at times but generally loved working with the kids.

My experience was tougher. My first day as a student chaplain at Boston City Hospital, one of the patients on my list to visit was a Puerto Rican in his early thirties who was laid up with a broken leg, which he had injured jumping off a bridge trying to commit suicide. He had inadvertently landed on two people, killing one of them, an elderly woman, and was now awaiting trial for manslaughter. Several others were in various stages of dying, and it was my job as a chaplain in the hospital to help them through the process. Almost everyone was destitute and in a hopeless situation. To say that I was in over my head is putting it mildly.

Particularly challenging for me were the small group-therapy sessions we had each day with two leaders and six participants, all men. The goal was to tear down our defenses and build us back up again. The main social defect that I had at the time—and still have, for that matter—was what one of the group leaders called "a severe case of naive, adolescent enthusiasm." He tried his best to rid me of this affliction through constant in-your-face confrontation. The scary thing was he came pretty close to succeeding.

In the group therapy, typically one person would be "on" for most of the ninety-minute session, which started each morning at 10:30. The job of the group was to get the person to acknowledge his various defense mechanisms and to be honest about his true feelings and "get in touch" with himself. The idea was to penetrate the various layers of defense mechanisms, often by confronting the person directly. Once each of us realized how uptight and defensive we were, we could grow and become better ministers.

At least that was the idea.

I got off pretty easy at first and was even somewhat shocked by the displays of emotion of my fellow participants. Toward the end of the summer, the question came up as to whether or not we hated our fathers. The seminary student next to me was the first to reply that yes, definitely, he did. I was a bit puzzled. The next guy did him one better, saying he hated his father's guts. Then one person broke down in tears. And so it went. When my turn came—I was the last to speak—I replied that I considered myself the lucky one of the group because actually I loved my father.

Suddenly all eyes were on me, and one of the leaders—a short, humorless man in his mid-thirties with a crew cut and an acute sense of when to go for the jugular, perked up and said, "Joe, the reason you say you love your father is because you hate him so much you can't even face it. This is what is holding you back and is probably one of the reasons for your naiveté and immaturity." It was now "my turn."

I can't remember how many days I was on after that, but it was at least for the better part of a week, and the troubling thing about it was that when you are alone facing a jury of five peers and two supposedly experienced leaders and they all say that you are not facing up to the truth, eventually you start to believe them. At least I did; and after three or four sessions I finally gave in, weeping as most of the others had done at one time or another, at which point I was embraced and hugged by various members of the group.

But while I admitted that, yes, I must hate my father like everyone else hated theirs, for the life of me I could not figure out why and never did. It took years for me to get over that experience and get back to the relationship I had enjoyed with my father before the group therapy experience.

Toward the end of the summer, the leader, half apologetically and half smugly, commented in passing, "You know, Joe, we have done a pretty good job tearing you apart. I'm sorry we don't have enough time to put you back together again."

The experience working at Boston City Hospital was for me a big, often painful, step in the process of growing up. One of the people I was assigned to minister to was a young woman about my age from a white, working-class family. She was quite overweight and her face looked more like that of someone in her forties than in her twenties. She had some relatively rare kind of cancer and her odds of surviving were slim. She suspected her disease was terminal and confided in me that though her family was nominally Catholic, she had no use for religion or the church and was terrified of dying. As far as I could tell, other than her mother, I was her only visitor. I was confused as to what my role should be, how much I should talk about religion and how much I should just be there for her. I opted for the latter approach, spending time with her each day, often hours, just sitting beside her bed. From what she told me, her life had been pretty grim from start to finish. She had been sexually abused by her stepfather at a young age, had never had a serious boyfriend, had had an abortion at age seventeen, dropped out of high school, and before entering the hospital was living at home, unemployed. In three weeks she was dead.

Her family asked me to officiate at the funeral, which was held in their modest row house in a rundown section of South Boston with a handful of weeping family members and neighbors seated around the casket in their small living room. It was the first, and last, funeral I ever performed.

A couple of days later Embry and I went out for dinner and a movie, *The Pawnbroker*, starring Rod Steiger, about a white pawnbroker in a Harlem neighborhood. The pawnbroker was callous and unfeeling, seemingly oblivious to the hardships experienced by the poor, usually desperate, black people he dealt with in his shop. He represented the kind of white racist that in my view at the time was one of the nation's major problems—uncaring, remote, hateful, and downright mean. Then as the movie began to unfold, little by little it became apparent that he had been a victim of the Nazi concentration camps and that his drab life in a small suburban bungalow on Long Island was not much better than the lives of his black customers in Harlem. The film did have a message of hope and redemption at the end, but the first time I saw it I missed that altogether. I was devastated.

I did not say a word as we left the theater; and then as I sat in the driver's seat of the car, I completely fell apart. Embry must have thought I was having a nervous breakdown, which I probably was. I must have sobbed uncontrollably for something like fifteen minutes before I finally regained my composure. The lives of the characters in the film were tragic—they experienced poverty, loneliness, isolation, torture, and despair. Then I thought of all the people I was trying to be a pastor to at the hospital. Their lives were not much better. How could a twenty-two-year-old woman with such a sad life die so young and so lonely? How could everyone I was ministering to be so poor? How could everyone be so unhappy, so lonely? Images flooded my brain: like Hector and Mary, the poor black woman that cold morning in Nashville, the bedraggled mother of five near the Tennessee prison, and the polio victims at Warm Springs. What was going on? Where was God in all this? What kind of God would permit the Holocaust, would permit such poverty and unhappiness? Where was justice? How could the world be so hard for some people, so tough, so unfair?

Suddenly, as if out of the blue, I realized that is just the way the world is. It is not *only* a world of suffering and pain, but when you look at reality squarely in the face, there is no denying that suffering and pain are very real. And at the end we all die. Though painful, the breakdown was a catharsis. It took several days to come to grips with it, but finally I did. Having faced what seemed to me the absolute tragedy of human existence, I said, OK, now that I understand this, I am going to move on. There are things people can do to make a difference, maybe not a lot, but life is worth living because that is all we have. But I never viewed the world in the same way again.

★★★

It was a summer of growing up in other ways as well. Just before we were ready to leave Boston, I popped the question to Embry. For some reason I chose Durgin Park, which was a famous restaurant in Quincy Market, located near the waterfront and known for its roast beef and family-style dining. When I made the decision to go to Durgin Park, I did not realize that we would be eating at a large table with a lot of people we did not know, but I figured, what the heck. So I asked the question and gave her the ring, to the astonishment of a half-dozen or so delighted dinner companions who were complete strangers. She accepted on the spot to smiles and toasts.

The marriage ceremony was held on December 28, 1965, during the middle of my second year in seminary, in the Davidson College Presbyterian Church, which was just about full—probably close to one thousand attendees. Embry's father, as president of a small college in a small town, was obliged to invite almost everyone, and almost everyone attended. Embry's uncle, Jack McMichael—her mother's brother and a Methodist minister—performed the ceremony. Jack was actually at Union himself for part of my first year, getting his PhD. He was one of a rare breed, a white southern radical, having been involved in numerous left-wing causes and summoned before the House Un-American Activities Committee during the Communist witch hunt in the 1950s. He could not have been a better fit for us.

In those days Davidson was "dry," so at the reception there was no alcohol offered to the guests, no dancing, and hardly any food. But it was a great occasion nonetheless, and most people found ways to enjoy themselves. My friends had brought in sufficient amounts of contraband to make it a real party for them, and I suspect plenty of others did the same. Not having any money, we spent our honeymoon week at Embry's parents' lake house about ten miles from the college.

I was very impressed with Embry's family. Her mother came from a quite unusual family in Quitman, Georgia, a small town not far from where Embry and I later worked in the civil rights movement. One of her aunts married an artist and lived in New York, and she and her husband supported left-wing causes while raising five artistic, nonconformist children. A second aunt, an even more infamous and eccentric nonconformist, lived in Richmond. Embry's mother, Louise, was probably the closest to normal of the family, though she was fundamentally as progressive and independent as her siblings. She was also the perfect college president's wife, taking an active and highly visible role in campus activities, earning her the love of faculty and students alike. The fourth sibling was "Uncle Jack," who married us.

Embry's father, Grier Martin, was a very effective and popular college president who supported the faculty, was accessible to students, and was a great fundraiser. He could often be found outside the main campus building tossing Frisbees with students. He positioned Davidson to make big changes in the late 1960s and 1970s—opening its doors to blacks and to women and broadening the faculty and the student body. Unlike his wife's family, composed of southern intellectuals and artists, Grier and his three brothers grew up on a farm near Atlanta and were entrepreneurs. Grier Martin was a good businessman, but not in any sense as driven as his brothers. As evidenced by his feeble attempt to persuade me to cancel the civil rights march in Charlotte, he and his wife secretly approved of what I was doing, which explains in part why they approved when their daughter married someone like me.

At about the time of our marriage, my father-in-law began to show signs of forgetfulness, ultimately resulting in his retirement in 1968, before he could see through the changes that he had initiated. He died in 1973 from Alzheimer's disease at age sixty-three.

★★★

I started the spring 1966 semester at Union a married man. Embry switched from Randolph-Macon to Barnard, where she was a math major, and we moved into the married section of the student dormitory in Hastings Hall, overlooking Broadway. The dorm had a central kitchen and men's and women's bathrooms, and everyone wheeled his or her cart down the hall to cook and wash dishes—probably not the ideal environment to start off a marriage but manageable given that it was really the only option available.

What had changed at Union for me in early 1966 when I returned from winter break and our abbreviated honeymoon was the presence of a new classmate named Charles Sherrod, an African American from Albany, Georgia. Charlie had been involved in the civil rights movement since the early 1960s and was an ordained Baptist minister. Charlie's main agenda seemed to be recruiting fellow students to work with him in the civil rights movement in Albany and surrounding areas in southwest Georgia during the upcoming summer. He talked about school desegregation and voter registration and how help from the outside was needed to make this happen. He was charismatic, focused, and very convincing, challenging us to put our faith into action and do what was right. Although we knew very few details about what would be involved in following him to Georgia, we had faith in Charlie. Embry was just as impressed with him as I was. We talked it over and decided to sign up. This was technically part of an initiative sponsored by the Student Interracial Ministry (SIM). SIM had been started at Union in 1960 by several seminary students who left Union to work in black churches in the South in order to promote interracial activities. But it was Charlie Sherrod, not SIM, who inspired us to go to southwest Georgia.

I did not know anything about Charlie's background when we made the decision to follow him. I later learned that he grew up in Petersburg, Virginia, part of a large family, and was raised mostly by his grandmother, who was a devout Baptist. As a child Charlie sang in the choir, attended Sunday school, and even occasionally was allowed to preach at his church. He got a degree from Virginia Union Seminary in 1961 and was ordained. He was older than me and most of my classmates—almost thirty.

While Charlie had protested segregation as early as 1954, when he and a black friend attended a white church uninvited, 1961 was the year he became involved in a big way. While a student at Virginia Union, he joined a sit-in in one of the Richmond department stores; and in 1961, my freshman year at Davidson, he participated in a sit-in in Rock Hill, South Carolina. He was arrested there, refused bail—one of the first to do this—and spent thirty days in jail. He had joined SNCC at its founding and was assigned the task of organizing the movement in southwest Georgia, where he moved in the fall of 1961 at age twenty-four. As the field secretary there from 1961 to 1967, he was one of the leaders who organized the 1961–62 protests in Albany. Unlike a lot of the civil rights activists who went from protest to protest and from battleground to battleground, Charlie stayed put and worked tirelessly behind the scenes to organize blacks in the small towns and rural counties in that part of the state. I was not exactly sure why Charlie was at Union, since he already was ordained, but I figured he probably was there to get a break from the action.

During the first five years of the civil rights movement, whites were not only welcomed but recruited by black leaders. The central message of the Haverford–Bryn Mawr conference had been "Help us," "Get involved." Whites were encouraged to come to Birmingham and to Selma and to work in Freedom Summer. It was important during that time that the movement be integrated, not exclusively black. During the spring of 1966, when we committed to going with Charlie along with several classmates, this was all starting to change.

At about the time of Selma there were inklings that the civil rights movement was going to start taking some different turns. A new crop of leaders in the movement were starting to emerge, and one of these was Stokely Carmichael. Born in Trinidad, he came to the United States as a child to join his working-class parents, who had immigrated to New York City some years earlier. He attended the prestigious Bronx High School for Science and then Howard University in Washington before joining SNCC in the mid-1960s. Carmichael was assigned to register voters in one of the toughest counties of all, Lowndes County, Alabama. He spearheaded a successful effort there and helped organize a new Democratic Party of African Americans to counter the white Democratic Party. The organization was called the Lowndes County Freedom Organization, and its symbol was the black panther. The symbol for the white Democratic Party was a white rooster. The changes that were beginning to happen were not yet apparent to many people outside of SNCC, but they would become a major factor in 1966—just at the time we were headed to southwest Georgia.

All this happened at the same time that the racial urban disturbances started. The first large outbreak took place in Watts in Los Angeles in 1965. The "riots" (a term many blacks disputed) were violent and disorganized but demonstrated the anger and frustration felt by many African Americans—and the potential power this anger could unleash. What we did not know was that the idea of moving from an integrated movement to an all-black movement was being fiercely debated within SNCC just at the time that Charlie was recruiting his white seminary friends to join him in Georgia. The idea of nonviolent civil disobedience was being replaced by "self-defense" and "black self-determination." Carmichael was the leader of the side that wanted to change direction. John Lewis, Bob Moses, and Charles Sherrod were on the other side. Carmichael won. But we did not know this before we got down there and were the first to experience what it meant. The first time the term "Black Power" was used publicly was by Stokely Carmichael in a speech in Greenwood, Mississippi, in June 1966, almost exactly the same time we were arriving in southwest Georgia.

★★★

This was the backdrop in the spring of 1966 as we were anxiously anticipating our trip south. We had no idea what we were getting ourselves into. We knew surprisingly little about what was happening in the civil rights movement. We believed in the cause. We believed in Charlie. We felt it was important to do our part. It was an expression of faith, a way of making a difference, the right thing to do. But as to what it was really all about, we were clueless.

The diary that follows begins with a description of the orientation conference we attended in Wake Forest, North Carolina, with over a hundred seminary students from various theological schools. The purpose was to prepare us for our summer fieldwork and internships. Those of us from Union were the only ones who were going to work in the civil rights movement. Most others would be working in traditional roles like counseling at religious summer camps, teaching, and helping with various church programs. The group that led the conference was the Ecumenical Institute, based in Chicago. They were described as "radical Christian leftists" who were dedicated to using radical organizing tactics in order for Christianity to take over the world. The approach of the conference was to break down our defenses in order to make us stronger warriors for Christianity.

This odd approach led to some humorous experiences. One occurred the morning of the second day, when all conference attendees were required to attend a 7:00 breakfast. A thin, bald man wearing a gray suit, white shirt, and thin tie, probably in his early thirties, came directly over to where I was sitting and suddenly yanked from his chair the man sitting next to me.

"What do you want on your tombstone? What do you want on your tombstone?" he screamed in the student's face.

Everyone stared in tense silence.

Very calmly the guy replied, "You want to know what I want on my tombstone, you really want to know? I want, 'Bury me upside down so you can kiss my ass,' you jerk."

I suppose I did not write these and other humorous events of this strange conference in my diary because humor was not on our minds back then. It was a pretty serious and pretty scary time, as we ventured into uncharted waters in the Deep South in hopes of making a difference.

PART II

Civil Rights Diary

with Embry Howell

Diary of
Joe Howell: Summer 1966

[*Except where otherwise indicated, notations in italics
are by Embry ("Mimy") Howell. Note that "Mimy"
was a nickname she dropped a few years later.*]

Wake Forest, North Carolina
June 2, 1966

W here to begin? A new summer and a new life—what will lie in
store?

A marriage—Mimy—a semester of hard study at Union.

Where am I now? Where am I going?

My present situation is one of certainty and uncertainty, but before I
try to focus on my own self-awareness, there is a more urgent experience
upon which to reflect.

It is the second day of the orientation and a large group of us has
walked out of the meeting. Having listened to the most ludicrous
distortion of theology by a doubtless well-meaning but blind and
mechanical phony from the Ecumenical Institute several of us protested
vociferously. The man denied that we had any right to question until
after the conference was over, so we walked out. Feaver [*Ed Feaver, a
classmate from Union Seminary and one of the leaders of the Student Interracial
Ministry (SIM)*] led the way. I followed; and behind us came virtually
the entire group. Three remained.

Now Mimy and I are sitting on the grass. She is reading *Manchild* [*Manchild in the Promised Land by Claude Brown, a popular book at the time about growing up black in the United States*]. I recently found out that while we went to find our books, Feaver and many of the others reentered. What does all this mean? My strong reaction was primarily against what I felt to be manipulation. I could not believe the opening lecture. The man spoke with "prerecorded" gestures and motions and wrote [*on the blackboard*] various statements that were absurd and which we were supposed to accept as "*the* authority." When denied the right to question, I, along with several others, felt I could not tolerate it.

This experience seems significant for several reasons. It shows how strongly we react against authority—in particular authority that is oppressive. Perhaps this attitude toward authority is one of our reasons for going to southwest Georgia in the first place.

It also shows, however, how necessary it is to have a leader—a person one respects and is willing to follow. We are going to need a leader this summer and Charlie is that leader.

June 4

The session for today is now over, and we are sitting under the trees in the late afternoon. The sun is an orange ball flooding the deep green campus of Wake Forest.

This has been the most unusual conference I have ever attended. Thursday afternoon we never returned to the meeting. After a great deal of turmoil and discussion, most of the Union contingent decided to continue with the program, using our free time to do the work that we thought was necessary. The most interesting thing that happened was the appearance of Jessie Harrison, a SNCC worker, who participated in our morning session. He is a short, very dark Negro from Alabama. [*The term "black" was only beginning to be used in 1966, as seen in the writings of Martin Luther King Jr. and others of that era; "Negro" was used to refer to black/African American people at that time; Joe usually uses the term "Negro" but sometimes "black," and I have left these terms as he used them, since it is interesting to see the change taking place as concepts of "Black Power" emerged that summer.*] He has the SNCC look—a spark in his eye, a broad smile, an arrogant defiance of all authority, self-assured, open, a great sense of humor. He is a beautiful person—I am continually amazed at his perceptiveness, self-awareness, and depth. Though a SNCC worker for the last six years, he does not follow the nationalist stance—he believes in helping people help themselves. It is too bad that he won't be with us this summer. He will be enrolling at the University of Wisconsin next year and is taking courses there this summer.

Thursday evening we went to another speech, which was much more emotional than the first one. After about ten minutes, the tall scrawny fellow was ranting and screaming and being laughed at by most of the participants. After forty-five minutes for me his performance changed from humorous to pathetic. His eyes bulged and his imagery became more coarse and sexual. The man is obviously psychopathic.

After an hour I walked out in disgust. I went directly to the chapel. It was the first time I prayed in a long while.

After the lecture, Mimy came out and we decided to skip the seminar in favor of going up the road with Tim and Susan Kimrey for a beer. The southwest Georgia group reassembled at 11:30 p.m. and met until after 1:00 a.m., discussing whether or not we should go our separate way from the Ecumenical Institute. David Hawk proposed to omit the planned program and substitute our own. Lots of emotional opinions were expressed on both sides; and a compromise—presented by Jessie Harrison of SNCC no less, he does not even have to be here!—was adopted that we would use most of the free time working on the particulars of the Southwest Georgia Project, with the rest of the participation being optional.

June 5

Mimy and I went to the opening meeting, an hour-and-a-half business session, where everyone in the entire conference—not just the Union people—was dealing with the same issue of whether to drop out or continue with the Ecumenical Institute's training session. This result was that each group would decide for itself whether or not it wanted to participate in the lectures and seminars. We stuck with our decision of the previous evening—the other two groups made similar choices. The lectures/seminars were declared optional. Mimy and I spent most of the day in town, lying in the shade of the trees.

That afternoon Sherrod arrived! He got there around noon and brought Seth, a white SNCC worker from Columbia, and Eddie Brown, a Negro SNCC worker from Albany, with him. Eddie had the "SNCC look"—handsome, proud, and cocky. Before Sherrod moved in [*into Albany, Georgia, to set up the Southwest Georgia Project*], rumors were that Eddie was a gang leader in Albany. Now he is a leader in the movement.

That afternoon Jessie, Eddie, Edith (a Negro girl from Smith), Robert (a Negro college student studying in Nashville), and I went up the road to buy some beer. I learned one of the first rules—always back your car in—never go in front ways [*presumably for safety reasons, in order to leave a place quickly if necessary*].

With Sherrod came the spirit we had all been anticipating. That afternoon Jessie and Eddie gave sketches of the area and several "dos" and "don'ts." The most important don't is never lead or give orders; always listen, encourage; the *local* people must do the work themselves. The important thing is for us to *listen*, to question, and to help the people *help themselves*. A lot of time was spent discussing our role with respect to the new SNCC position on independent organization, called by some "black nationalism." The word we got from Jessie and Eddie was "Don't sweat it man, there's still a lot you can do. But it ain't gonna be any picnic." Charlie spoke, too, but only to comment on what the others had said. They were extremely articulate, free, and sensitive people. Very impressive human beings!

That evening this spirit really caught on. All of a sudden we were all happy, and after dinner the spirit burst forth in freedom songs. Some started singing "Oh, Freedom" [*one of the most popular songs from the civil rights movement*], and for thirty minutes the auditorium really rocked. The charisma of Sherrod is incredible.

June 6

We got about five hours of sleep Friday night (four the night before!) and spent Saturday morning in the final EI meeting, which was devoted to organization building, and not too bad. There was some helpful information amid the usual propaganda.

After lunch and a communion service, most of the people departed and went their separate ways. We took a couple of hours and tried to get some sleep, in order to be half awake for the evening trip to Albany. We woke up around 5:15 p.m. and by 6:00 p.m. were ready to go. Since there were ten of us in two cars, we decided to drive down staying together. At 8:00 we finally left.

Larry, Mickey, Chris, John, Mimy, and I were in one car. Feaver, Joe Pfister, Bill Kownover, and Larry Mamiya were in the other. The trip was long but enjoyable. At 5:30 in the morning the sun rose and we found ourselves in southwest Georgia.

Albany, Georgia
June 7

As we neared Albany, Feaver drove us through Vienna and Cordele, showing us the general area. The Negroes live in extreme poverty. The whites who are at the lowest economic level are only a few notches higher. There are many beautiful houses and large farms—some tobacco and cotton, and a great deal of corn and peanuts. We saw many gigantic fields of peanuts and many groves of pecan trees.

As we got further south, the country grew even more beautiful— Spanish moss grew from huge oak trees. Many trees and flowers were in bloom, etc.

Completely exhausted, we got into Albany, 229½ Jackson St. [*the offices of the Southwest Georgia Project and SNCC*], at 10:30 a.m. The rest of the group had arrived at 2:00 a.m. Everyone looked beat.

The SNCC office is eight rooms—quite dirty and disorganized. The walls of the main room are covered with various pictures and souvenirs of the movement: civil rights posters, maps, segregationist signs, flags, photographs, etc. Two rooms serve for office work, three for sleeping, and two for a library. Generally, the place has an atmosphere of intrigue about it. One feels as if a revolution is under way.

We had another meeting of "orientation" where the SNCC workers, Isaac and Randy, did most of the talking. Nothing new was said: more warnings about police brutality and more on independent organizing. Apparently, we will be in three or four counties. The SNCC people will be working with Black Power in Clay, Calhoun, and Mitchell [*Counties*], and we are not to interfere there. Six of us will work in the Head Start program in Baker, five in Albany, and three or four in Cordele. [*This was the second summer of the national Head Start program, and we were integrating the program in order to meet national guidelines for receiving money.*] What we will be doing is uncertain, although Sherrod emphasized voter registration, political education, the welfare problem (Negroes not getting proper aid), and Head Start. ASCS [*Agricultural*

Stabilization Conservation Service] elections are coming up, as are general elections, so voter registration will be a main thrust.

The problem is, however, that the SNCC workers are not sure of their own position toward us. Isaac and Randy both were open and very articulate and did not seem to be hostile. But they certainly were not overjoyed to see us either. Apparently, a deal has been worked out between SNCC and Sherrod, the result of which is that SNCC will *tolerate* us, at least for a while. [*We did not know it at the time but Sherrod had had a major falling out with Stokely Carmichael, who had taken over—some would say usurped—the SNCC leadership and Charlie had distanced himself from the SNCC national organization.*]

That afternoon, we went to Baker County. Unbelievably beautiful country—many large plantations, swamps, trees covered with Spanish moss. We played basketball at the Millers' and went to a mass meeting that evening. The meeting was held at an old church seemingly in the wilderness at 7:30 p.m. By 9:30 p.m., about twenty farmers had arrived, mostly men, and good solid people. [*In Georgia that summer we began referring to "Baker County time," and ever since it has been our term for casual timekeeping.*] My reaction was that they were much nearer to white farmers than they were to SNCC workers in terms of general attitude about life (although of course they shared experiences of racism). I was half asleep, having had about two hours' sleep in the car and no dinner. By 10:45 p.m. the meeting was over, and we returned home to Albany. (Mimy and I had thought we would stay in Baker, but the time "wasn't right." Too much fear. The farmers seemed a little wary of us.)

Mimy and I had to split up in the evening. She stayed at a friend of Charlie's with Ellen. Luckily, around midnight I struck up a conversation with an Albany State College student who invited me to stay with him. Romberg was there, too. It was a nice apartment, and I slept until 10:30 the next morning. We had a good breakfast with the guys (Willie Edwards and William Walker) and did some talking about school, civil rights, and things in general.

June 8

The SNCC office is in the center of "Harlem," the Negro section of Albany—above a pool hall. My first reaction is that the similarities to Harlem in New York City are greater than the differences—open bars, lots of drinking, hollering, horn blowing, swearing, shooting pool, talk of sex, etc. The difference is that in Albany there is only one street like this, and we are in the center of it. The evening before last at 3:00 a.m. when we could not get to sleep (on the floor of a hot, dirty room in the SNCC headquarters) because of all the hollering outside, I felt like we were back in New York City.

Nothing eventful happened in the afternoon. We spent most of the time around the SNCC office talking to the workers.

The SNCC workers are a strange breed. I have never seen anything quite like them: cocky, proud, lots of rough language. [*Not around me, only around Joe.*] On the one hand, they remind me of a Harlem gang. On the other hand, they are extremely bright and articulate and have a purpose—even if it is somewhat uncertain. I can't blame them for being cynical and distrustful toward white people. They have an attitude toward us that seems ambivalent. We are whites and consequently the oppressors; yet we are there to help. We are religious—at least they think we are. They are extremely bitter and cynical about the church. They talk "bop" talk, and walk what I would call a Harlem "jive." Whites are "white cats" if they are OK. Most whites, however, are "crackers." Negroes are usually just "cats." "Man" is used in every sentence. "Like" is used a lot. They are a strange sort of people. Right now I feel they are good people and have a reason for being here.

Isaac: The project chairman, very young (eighteen or nineteen), immature, but very bright. He is not on top of things, nor is he the real leader. Basically a good, solid person, but too inexperienced and unsure of himself. He has a great deal of potential but does not command enough respect from the others to be an effective leader.

Grady: When I first met Grady his only comment was, "Goddamn, man, it looks like the roosters outnumber the panthers. Panthers are hungry. Panthers *eat* roosters." He calls himself Grady 3X and looks and talks like Malcolm X. He is very loud, aggressive, and says he hates whites. He does not talk to whites and has made it clear he does not want us in southwest Georgia. Grady finds his identity with national SNCC and is a party man all the way. Apparently, he is one of the leaders of SNCC, and he tells Isaac what to do. I'm not sure what Grady has done in a local movement anywhere. I don't think he has done much.

Hermon: Grady's best friend. He has a freer mind than Grady and does not mind admitting that he is wrong. He does not like whites either and does not want us there—but for reasons that are more pragmatic than ideological. Right now our being there will mess up their organizing independent Black Power. Hermon is extremely vocal, hostile, and I must admit, rather threatening. I think I would like to get to know him better, though there does not seem to be much room for communication.

John Baptiste: Very light skinned, with long curly brown hair and hazel eyes. Baptiste has been in the movement much longer than any of the other SNCC workers and is a tremendous human being. He is brilliant and articulate and is very different from the other SNCC workers. He is an independent thinker and stands apart from any SNCC party line. He believes in the Black Power emphasis as a pragmatic goal and consequently does not want us in Clay, Calhoun, or Baker! He is not antiwhite but "anticracker"—and seems to know the difference between the two. He has a deep sensitivity for helping poor people of any color.

Baptiste is from low country South Carolina, has spent a quarter at Antioch College and some time at Howard University. He rebelled against the middle-class apathy of both colleges and did not stay with it long enough to graduate. He has serious stomach problems (ulcers and no telling what else) and has not been feeling well.

Randy: Another independent person, but quite different from Baptiste. Randy is the kind of guy who says exactly what is on his mind and makes no apologies to anyone. He tells you that the guys in SNCC are a bunch of phonies and don't do a goddamn thing. He tells you he hasn't done a hell of a lot himself. "Yeah, I worked for SNCC for a year and a half. It was a paid vacation, man." I'm not sure what his role is in the movement. He says he is leaving next week for New York, then San Francisco, then South America. We played pool yesterday for a couple of hours and tied 4-4.

Eddie Brown: He wears funny clothes and sunglasses. Probably about my age. Rough, handsome, and wild. He is also a unique person and very different from the other guys. He was previously a gang leader in Albany and was recruited into SNCC by Sherrod. He is still a hell-raiser and is free from any real allegiances. He seems more authentic in his use of jive talk than the other guys (except perhaps Randy)—and has a beautiful sense of rhythm in his speaking. He reminds me of the fellows I worked with on the Lower East Side in New York—strong, rebellious, compulsive, and uncontrollable. He is a local person and very much a part of the city life in Albany. His way of life is much nearer to the New York style than it is to any southern agrarian style. Apparently he makes many trips to New York.

There are other people besides the SNCC staff who are very involved in the movement. So far we have met only Rev. Fulwood of Cordele, an articulate and powerful speaker. He did a tremendous job chairing the long meeting Monday evening and is the leader of the Cordele movement. He has been criticized by some in SNCC for being a "black God." He has a great deal of self-awareness and speaks freely of his feelings against the SNCC workers. According to Feaver, his main handicap is that he is erratic and not always dependable, but Feaver says he is basically a very good man.

Ramona is a beautiful, quiet Negro girl who wears her hair very short (in the "natural African style"). She is Baptiste's girl and a person I would like to know better. It is rumored that Baptiste is going to marry Ramona—but he has never admitted that this is true.

That evening was the "showdown" meeting between "Sherrod's volunteers" and the SNCC workers. Everyone knew something had to happen, because there had been an extremely hostile attitude toward us the whole time. Isaac, Hermon, and Grady went to the Atlanta office. When they returned, the meeting began, five hours after the scheduled time. From 9:00 p.m. until 1:00 a.m. we all sat squeezed into a hot sticky room. Fulwood chaired the meeting, and one by one the SNCC workers let us have it.

The first issue was over Baker County and how Sherrod had broken his truce by letting us go into the county the previous evening when we attended a mass meeting. SNCC did not want white people "messing around" in Baker County. The climax came when Grady got up and shouted that he didn't want whites at all in the movement; and if those in Baker interfered in what he was doing, he would "smother them." He said he and Hermon were the sneakiest guys in southwest Georgia and could smother anyone. Someone echoed that if any one of us white folks participated in the Baker County movement, it would be "foot in ass" for us.

Sherrod came back and made the distinction between whites and crackers and how he was anticracker, but not antiwhite. After more discussion, I asked who we were to take orders from, the local people or from the SNCC staff, and if they wanted us to help with voter registration, what we should do. Another heated debate followed, with Grady saying I proved his point that all white men were stupid and didn't know what they were doing. The talk went on and on. The Baker County issue was finally resolved by the fact that white people were needed to get fifty thousand dollars from the federal government on the Head Start program. So we must go, but we were to work *only* on Head Start. If we were asked to do other things, it was agreed we could, so long as we stayed away from the Black Panther movement. [*As I recall, there was no more mention of the Black Panthers all summer once we settled in Baker County.*] We had won the battle. We were going into Baker.

Similar battles took place that night over Cordele, and hostility arose among the SNCC workers. Grady made fun of Fulwood. Fulwood got mad. Fulwood and Joe, the white worker, got into a verbal battle, etc. etc.

By one o'clock in the morning everybody had gotten a chance to say what was on their mind, and all of a sudden things seemed OK. It was the strangest thing. Everything had been said. The hostility was out in the open. Communication was reestablished.

We all stood up and sang some songs. Sherrod began a spiritual, and everyone joined in. Then came "Oh, Freedom." It felt great to be alive.

Mimy and I spent another night on the floor of the SNCC office. It was hot and noisy. We did not get to sleep until 3:00 a.m.

June 9

It was a long, hard, and frustrating day. Everyone had gone to Cordele but Ellen, Mimy, and I, and there was nothing for us to do. We talked to Baptiste for an hour, went to the laundromat, and generally just hung around the office.

We spent a couple of more hours talking with Baptiste, Hermon, and Eddie. Hermon apologized for his rough remarks to me Monday evening and was very open and friendly. They are uncompromising radicals and are distrustful of everything from Martin Luther King and SCLC to federal poverty funds to Head Start programs. Any compromise to them is wrong. Last year Hermon was offered a twelve-thousand-dollar-a-year job [*quite a nice, middle-class salary in 1966*] with the antipoverty program and turned it down, remaining on an eight-hundred-dollar-a-year SNCC subsistence salary.

Baptiste was also offered ten thousand dollars in the antipoverty program and rejected it. Last year all the SNCC workers were supposedly offered college scholarships by various colleges. No one accepted. According to them, any part of the present system is evil; and if anyone becomes a part of it, he, too, is corrupted. Hermon and Baptiste cited examples of SNCC workers who had been "bought off" by the federal government and now were doing nothing but mailing letters at twelve thousand dollars a year. The system can't be changed from within.

The lives that these guys have led are quite amazing. Take John Baptiste. From our conversation yesterday, I found out that we are the same age. When I was ten years old, Baptiste had left his home in low country South Carolina with some friends and gone to Cape Cod. He had met a Catholic priest there who had returned with him. Because Baptiste lived with the priest, the priest's car was bombed, windows shot out in his house, and a cross burned in his yard. Barely escaping death, Baptiste at age twelve left home for good.

For the next three years he wandered around Massachusetts from place to place, most of the time alone—working and studying part time. He went to a Catholic school for a while, but at age fourteen he got "fed up with the discipline" and left for Chicago. There he worked and went to night school, living in various places around the city. When the gang he was a part of beat up an old man and smashed his guitar, he knew that he had to cut out, so he left—without notice—for New York.

In New York City he lived with his brothers, who were spread out, in Harlem, the Bronx, and the East Village. He bummed around and finally managed to finish high school, taking his final year in upstate New York.

At age eighteen he left for Wisconsin, where he ran into a "streak of luck" (he would not say what this was) and later met a rich woman who gave him a scholarship to Antioch College. There was a controversy over race there, and after a quarter he and fifteen other Negroes left. He then went to Howard in Washington, D.C., where he managed to get a part-time job as a car salesman, earning $450 a week. Staying at Howard for a couple of years, he got fed up with the "black bourgeois" attitude and became interested in SNCC. In 1963 he participated in the March on Washington, which caused him to be fired from his job. He then left school for good and went to work for SNCC full time. We were both twenty-one years old in 1963. I had just completed my junior year at Davidson.

In the evening we attended the mass meeting in Albany at Mt. Zion Baptist Church, an old brick building probably built before the turn of the century. As in Baker County, the meeting started over an hour late, and only a handful of people were present. It was a hot, sultry evening, and all the fans were going. Because the chairman, Rev. Wells, was gone to Alabama, Sherrod chaired the meeting. One of the deacons led in a spiritual hymn, which even though fewer than twenty-five people were present seemed to shake the rafters. One elderly lady sitting about three pews in front of us had one of the most beautiful voices I have ever heard.

The meeting lasted about an hour and a half, the latter part being a goodbye speech by Dennis Roberts, attorney C. B. King's assistant [*King was a prominent civil rights lawyer in Albany and an associate of Martin Luther King—though no relation*]. He spent most of the time praising C. B. King as one of the greatest constitutional lawyers in the nation and noted five important projects: a credit union, welfare investigations, voter registration, equal employment opportunity, and equal representation on juries.

The spirit in Albany is not very high. The movement has gradually slowed to pretty much of a standstill. The people said they could do nothing without Rev. Wells, who has been in Alabama for several months. Several people got up and said something must be done. They must get moving again. No definite plans were suggested except that meetings will now be weekly instead of every other week.

Sherrod made pleas to house the volunteers; and, thank God, one couple agreed to help. So Mimy and I got a bed to sleep in that evening. Two nights on the floor of the SNCC office was enough for us. The couple's name is Meyers. They are both forty-nine years old and come from the farms in Richland County. [*At the time I remember them as being very old!*] Mr. Meyers is a lift driver at the Marine base and makes $2.17 an hour. Mrs. Meyers works as a maid. They have four grown children, all of whom are gone, and five grandchildren.

The Meyerses' house consists of two bedrooms and a tiny kitchen and is immaculate. There is no dust on the floor, and every piece of furniture and decoration is neatly in its place. The general style of the home reminds me of my grandmother's. There is a small toilet built on the side of the house and no hot water. Mimy and I slept in the front bedroom, which has just enough room for a TV and a double bed. We are very, very lucky.

Reflections:

So much has happened and I have so many thoughts—but they are often mixed up and confused.

All this is new and very different and somewhat threatening. It is not "middle-class," it is really different, it is strange. The situation here is complex and hard to put a finger on.

My general impression of SNCC is that they aren't really on top of things. Things actually are in a mess here. Are they really concerned about the local people? They have very little to do with the Albany movement. No one at the SNCC office knew where (or if!) the evening meeting was to be held. No one seemed to really care. Apparently their main task is to open up new counties, but whether or not they have actually done much during the past few years is hard to tell. My impression is that there is a lot more talk than action.

The SNCC workers are "full of shit" themselves if you ask me. Most people just hang around the office and shoot the bull. They have something on the ball, but they, too, are as messed up as us white folks. The "jive talk" is OK, but what are they really all about? It seems they (Isaac, Hermon, Grady, and Randy) form a kind of club or "in group." Ellen [*who was white*] thinks she's part of it, using all the four-letter words and talking about sex and how bad the whites are.

Who *are* the leaders? What is going on? What is the purpose? Charles Sherrod is a leader and a giant. I will follow him wherever he wants me to go. I respect him and love him. Fulwood of Cordele is a leader. He has a lot on the ball and is critical of the SNCC workers. But the others? What are they all about?

Baker seems to be doing better with local leaders. [*Baker County, while having several very large plantations with many poor, tenant farmers, was also blessed with many independent black farmers, who had owned their land for generations.*]

And where do *we* fit in? Obviously the SNCC people do not want us here—not because of the movement so much as because we threaten their leadership. I think these guys have found an identity and purpose in SNCC but don't really give a damn about the people.

But do *I*? What are Mimy and I doing here? Who are we to follow? Who are we here to "help"? There seems to be so little structure and so few people who really want us here. So if nobody wants us here—especially the people we have come down here to help—then why are we here in the first place?

Whoever said God is working through the civil rights movement has obviously not spent a lot of time in it. There are no idols. People are people everywhere. Humans are all in the same boat. No one is better because of participation in a great cause. Even Sherrod is human though I would like to make him into a god.

"Hang loose, man." That's the only way to survive. Be open—listen—learn—accept these people. We are as phony as they are. Let the Holy Spirit work.

June 10

This afternoon we met with SCLC group. In the evening in a rainstorm we drove to Sylvester in Worth County for a mass meeting. Only about twenty people were there, but a lot of people spoke up, especially the men. The basic issue was over the Head Start program, which had been refused funding by the OEO [*Office of Economic Opportunity, the federal agency in charge of the antipoverty program*] because the children weren't sufficiently integrated. Also, because only one Negro had applied to work on the board for distribution of food, a plea was made for more applications. It was a good meeting with lots of spirit. Wells made a dramatic appeal for the farmers to support us, and two men volunteered to house four of the white civil rights workers.

June 11

We are still at the Meyerses' house. We slept late and had a great breakfast of bacon, grits, and biscuits.

Among other things, Mr. Meyers is an avid news watcher. He watches the news every morning from 7:45 and every evening from 6:00 to 7:30. By switching channels, he is able to get two networks and three local news broadcasts. Although he has a ninth-grade education, he is one of the best-informed human beings I have ever met.

Mr. Meyers is extremely moral and very proud. He talks of what has been done in Albany and repeats he's not afraid of white folks. Dr. Martin Luther King is his hero (pictures of King and President Kennedy hang in their bedroom), and he loves Sherrod. He pulls out various cards from time to time and shows them to us—his union card, his work card, his voting card. Mr. Meyers calls himself a politician; and although he has never run for any office that is what he is. He loves people and life and is filled with enthusiasm. All this finds its focus on the news, elections, and government. Maybe someday he will be able to hold office.

After chatting with the Meyerses, we walked around the Negro residential section of Albany. The two people Mrs. Meyers thought we should see were Mrs. Slaytor King and Mrs. Jackson. Slaytor King (C. B.'s brother) has his real estate office in the same building with his brother—a very attractive, modern one-story building on South Monroe. We went there first to see Mrs. King, who works in her husband's office. She is a very attractive woman, probably in her late thirties, sophisticated and a very fashionable dresser. She is just one of the many beautiful Negro women that I have seen here. Perhaps this is personal growth for me. I never before was truly aware of the beauty of Negro people.

Mrs. King confirmed our awareness that the movement did not seem to be "moving" anywhere in Albany, but she said there was much activity in the antipoverty program and the Head Start program. She suggested we go by the community center, which we did, spending about an hour there. The center was very impressive—a large, old frame house converted into a recreation center with a ping-pong room, sewing center, meeting rooms, play rooms, etc. Mrs. Jackson told us about the $102,000, federally funded local antipoverty program, which includes the Head Start program and a tutoring program, under Mrs. C. B. King. All of these programs are well integrated and very large, and there is much excitement about them. She gave us some ideas to research for her about starting a federal savings bank which would serve the Negro community. Much more is going on at 401 S. Madison [*the community center*] than at 229½ S. Jackson [*the SNCC office*]!

We walked to the SNCC office and spent a couple of hours talking with Baptiste and Hermon. At 4:30 Eddie drove us back to the Meyerses' house via the South Jackson community center. We drove through much of the poor Negro section of town. Some of the dwellings are shacks, resting on bricks (with garbage underneath), and some are newly painted (though old) with grass, gardens, and flowers. In some areas, Negroes live in very nice brick "suburban" homes, and in some cases the homes appear to be very expensive. Just from driving through the residential section you become very much aware of the class levels within the Negro community. This is another fact that previously I was only vaguely aware of.

That evening we went bowling with Ed, Charles, Wallace, and Joe Pfister.

June 12

Back from Hank's wedding. Great to see Hank, Sam, Reese, Killer, Young, and Keith. They are wonderful human beings. Hank married a very pretty girl, and I am very happy for him. [*The wedding was in Tallahassee. Hank Ackerman married Mell Laird. Forty years later Mell is still very pretty, and most of these folks—Joe's college classmates—are still our close friends.*]

[*Joe obviously wrote the following as an evening mass meeting in Baker County was under way, hence the telegraphic style.*]

Baker County: Sunday mass meeting. Around one hundred people. More women than men. Women up front and men in the rear. Men drift in. Meeting begins at 9:15 p.m., hours behind schedule.

Discussion over who would run for Board of Ed. Elderly farmer withdrew. Need to name a candidate. Need to try. The Millers, sitting together, give a strong plea. Mrs. Josie Miller was nominated. She'll do anything to help Baker County. "Let white men know we got some power." Another woman agrees to run. Mr. Broadway would run if he could keep his job in the civil service. Seven hundred [*black*] registered voters in Baker. [*In the 1960s Baker was a very sparsely populated county—as it still is today. The county had about forty-five hundred inhabitants, a figure that had declined to about four thousand in the 2000 census. Twenty-five hundred of the county's residents were black in the 1960s, so only about a quarter of the black population was registered to vote. Nearly fourteen hundred whites were registered to vote in Baker County, nearly the entire white population.*] Sherrod suggested that we set up a special committee for recruiting candidates and that we have a special strategy meeting.

Church is sweltering. Fans waving. [*The paper fans in the pews of all southern churches at the time, black and white.*] Murmuring. Little babies crawling. Children squirming. Old folks fanning. Men quiet. Women active. Different from last week when fewer people were present.

Hard time getting volunteers to help Mrs. Miller. Three men decline. More murmurs. Minutes drift away. Meeting next Wed. changed to Tues. One man bowls on Wed.

The civil rights struggle is long, slow, and hard. People in the South move and talk slowly.

Mrs. Holt [*Dovanna Holt, the person we were later assigned to live with for most of the summer—a very wonderful, warm, and strong woman*] speaks forcefully on getting volunteers (us?) a place to stay. Plans for renting a house. Long discussion. (Hard to follow. What house? For whom?)

Isaac speaks. They had planned for Negro college students to work there. He'll get the students tomorrow—four. Independent, *Black* Power. Sherrod speaks on new SNCC position. People hushed. Sherrod says he *was* against it [*i.e., having whites work in Baker*]. Whites in white communities. Only Negroes in Baker. That was the way to go. "You know my position. . . . I had agreed not to send in whites, but when I was asked about Head Start needing to be integrated, I thought it would be good to have these whites. . . . only for *that* reason did I go against SNCC. I thought people here *wanted* these whites in order to get the federal Head Start funding. And if they did come, they would have to stay in people's houses."

Only sound is baby sucking a bottle.

Mrs. Miller speaks, then Windy Roberts. Says it is good. Mrs. Holt speaks: "If these people are down here with no protection, anything could happen. It they are gonna work with us, I'm willing to share. It'll be better for us in the future, even if it's bad now. The Lord is blessing me. I'm going along with it—if *they* are willing. . . ."

Man speaks out. "We had a lot of trouble last year. . . . Something would happen to *me* before it would happen to *them*. They should stay in *their own* house. . . . Too risky."

Many fears come out. Several people leave.

Isaac says SNCC doesn't hate whites but needs for Negroes to stick together. SNCC people will live in the SNCC house. Should everyone live in SNCC house or everyone in the community? "If you take these whites, and not Negroes, you are discriminating."

More talk—pro and con. Danger. Women speak out for housing us and not SNCC. Time passes. Motion to let those stay in SNCC house who want to. But Mrs. Miller says her doors are wide open. Things are better this year. "We are 'quainted with whites. Lord's gonna see us through. Nobody shot us last year. Each family takes one person."

More fears about taking us.

Half the people have drifted out. Disunity. No idols in the movement. The difficulty of local people taking leadership. Sherrod keeps quiet. The people must decide.

More talk.

Mrs. Holt tells how much they enjoyed the Tampa Head Start program. "We felt so good and so free. We liked never to come back. We are doing the right thing. We are improving ourselves. We are helping our people." She is proud.

Mrs. Miller: "The Lord is with us. We learned so much from all these high educators. One day our children will talk right. Our children have problems. The government is backing us up. They were high educated, but talked so us uneducated could understand. I enjoyed it. So inspiring. . . Changes have come."

Another woman speaks. She wished she could rear her children again. "I felt so proud. Black people talked so good. I felt so good."

Other women smile. Fourteen attended the conference. They spent the hour before the meeting laughing and smiling. They are proud people.

Sherrod speaks for youth center and for using poverty funds for the movement. C. B. King's assistant tells of plan to get rid of Sheriff Warren Johnson [*the hated and feared sheriff of Baker County*] by sworn affidavits.

More talk about how white people in the county have been meeting and planning [*in anticipation of the antipoverty program funds coming into Baker*]. Man speaks of a call from a white man [*from the federal government*] who called nine men in the movement. Said he wanted to have a meeting with them to find what they (Negroes) really wanted. Desire to give Negroes what they want. Mrs. Miller cries out, "Freedom!"

They [*the local black men who had been invited*] met among themselves. The meeting was to have been last Friday but was put off because the sheriff couldn't make it.

Sherrod replies: "Here are white folks picking out people to represent the black community. It happened they did call many of our leaders, but they did not come to the movement. Women are also in the movement. *They* weren't invited. White folks can't make no decisions for the Baker County movement! Only you can make these decisions." The meeting ends with "We Shall Overcome."

June 13

[*Apparently Joe was also taking the following notes during a staff meeting the next day.*]

Sitting in the SNCC office, singing Negro spirituals with our entire group and several of the local young people (Jo Ann, Pat, etc.). Then we began going over current developments:

Albany: Feaver speaks on the credit union. Seven can apply (up to 100). Who: groups with a common interest, e.g., the movement. Apply to fed. credit union for charter. 25+ membership. The seven draw up rules and elect a board (5). Local credit unions can form into leagues, pooling resources.

How it works: Purpose is to get people to save. Shares cost $5. Encourage the "civic minded" who have money to put the money into the CU, not into stock, bonds, or banks. The manager must be bonded. Manager and bookkeeper are employed.

When credit union has $7,500, it can lend $750 without security (up to 10% of the CU's capital in loans). Withdrawals at will. Loans are 1% interest per month, max of 12% for year. Reserves cover bad loans.

Groups who can form CUs: (1) factories/businesses; (2) organizations (e.g., churches); (3) population groups, e.g., towns. "The movement" won't be accepted, but if the OEO backs it, it could get a charter. It has to be part of a Community Action Program (CAP), which has to be integrated. In CUs it is one man, one vote. If whites won't go along with it, then Negroes can apply alone with explanation.

One opinion: "Part of the antipoverty program salaries should be given to the movement. The program is corrupt at the core; and when it filters down, it is corrupt. We must fight *it*, too."

Pfister [*Joe Pfister was a fellow seminarian from Union*] speaks on his plan for a folk festival. Sherrod clarifies idea: There are people who don't have pride in the Negro heritage. They are ashamed. "The attempt is to give the local artists a platform on which to use their art." Sherrod cites examples of Negro talent—a cat who plays the Jew's harp, a blind singer, etc. etc. This is talent and is good. "Use *local* talent. Don't call in nothing. We don't need outsiders. This should include readings, rock and roll, rhythm and blues, spirituals, drama, dancing, art display, a cooking contest. . . . Keep your eyes open for any of this. Date: July 2. [*I do not remember this ever happening; and as I look at Joe's entry for July 2, I see no mention of it.*]

ASCS [*The organization responsible for crop allotments*] selection: Farmers are paid for not planting. Each county has an ASCS office. District elections for each office. No Negroes on ballots. Ballots mailed out. Before this happens, thirty days to petition for men to be on the ballot. The people who are elected decide who plants what. (One man from each district.) Whites have been able to plant; Negroes have not. Cotton, peanuts, tobacco are allotted. Corn, watermelons are not. Anyone over eighteen on a farm can vote: farmers, tenants, sharecroppers, landowners can vote; but you have to farm to vote. One vote per worksheet. Laborers can't vote.

Many Negroes never get ballots. Federal government allots county so many acres. Local ASCS board decides how the allotment goes.

In Baker there are three districts. Five men per district are elected. Chairman goes to county ASCS. Names on ballot can be written in. Need for more information. The need is to get Negroes on the ballot. Need for black block vote. Mass meeting in which everyone writes in same man. Still much uncertainty here.

Denis Roberts: Lawsuit against Sheriff Johnson. Early lawsuit lost. New kind of suit: Johnson is unfit for office. His intimidation has destroyed all the Negroes' efforts for injunction to keep him from further intimidation. This probably won't be won in federal court, but it will harass him and humiliate him, and hopefully be of therapeutic value.

We want to start talking to people. Get lists of stories. Figure out which stories would show Johnson's pattern, i.e., which families have been harassed, beaten, which relatives are afraid to visit and which people Johnson has abused and punished; people forget. It will be a long process. Keep pushing. Get other names. The purpose is to paint an accurate picture of Johnson and his henchmen: collect affidavits, select witnesses.

Ask questions first. Then go over the affidavits a second time. Then go over them a third time. He should be sure they are right. This man [*the one giving the affidavit*] must sign his name before a notary. If the man can't sign his name, we write his name. He must touch the pencil while we write. Above his name, he makes an "X." We write above the X, "his mark." We may write our name under his as a witness. This is not necessary. Work fast. See Bob Cover, C. B.'s summer assistant from Columbia U.

Isaac reports a Negro preacher was shot in Terrill County last Saturday night. Konover said the preacher in his church said Negroes there were near rioting.

★★★

The other questions discussed were individual job responsibilities and the work in the counties. All the counties are at a standstill. The Cordele movement has been virtually destroyed by the spring boycott and the "flag incident," which hurt everyone and helped no one. Rev. Fulwood and Ramona assume too much leadership and apparently dictate (especially Fulwood) over the natural local leaders, Deacon Burch and Mr. Cheeks. No local people have responded to the call for a march and none came to the last mass meeting. No churches will permit the movement to even use their churches. The SNCC freedom house has the reputation of being a brothel. Generally the movement has an image of being led by reckless, hell-raising sex maniacs who don't give a damn about the local Negroes. Matters are in bad shape there.

Yet there is so much that needs to be done, especially in the area of voter registration. The local people's confidence must be regained, and this will be a long, slow task. McInroy, Bill Konover, Dave Hawk, and Larry Mamiya have that very difficult responsibility.

Feaver, Jim Romberg, and Joe Pfister will be the first whites going into Worth County, where they will be working on the first intensive effort for voter registration. It will probably be dangerous.

It is still uncertain who will go with Mimy and me into Bad Baker. Besides teaching Head Start, we will be working on drives to collect affidavits against Sheriff Johnson, to get Negroes to file jury applications, to get Negroes to elect a black man on the ASCS board, to get a credit union started, and possibly to register voters. We'll be busy. [*I do not remember doing any of those jobs, other than Head Start and voter registration at the end. These tasks also conflicted with the explicit instructions to stay involved only in Head Start and leave the organizing to the SNCC workers.*]

Charles Wallace (the guy from Yale) is currently the only one of us to work in Albany. So far nothing much has been going on there.

The meeting adjourned for lunch and convened again at 1:30, lasting until 4:30. The tiny SNCC room was packed with people sweating in the thick heat. It was not a good meeting. A lot was said, but not much was resolved.

There was another mass meeting in Albany in the evening, which twenty-six local people plus two whites from the Marine base attended. Rev. Wells made another fiery speech in which he told people what to do. He is able to turn the emotion on and off like a water faucet, and consequently comes through to me as a phony. I also react very negatively toward what seem to me to be dictator-like tactics. He does not let the people decide for themselves. He does not leave room for discussion or the spontaneity which is natural in the Negro community. [*Joe: Rev. Wells was actually a hero of the civil rights movement in Albany, which began in November 1961 and lasted for almost a year but had run out of steam after that time and by 1966 was pretty dead.*]

Sherrod offered a plan for involvement and reported on the shooting of the minister in Dawson. The movement seems to be at a low ebb in Albany, with little ostensible spirit. Wells is a member of SCLC and is a living example of differences in philosophy between SNCC and SCLC. SCLC dictates from the higher ranks of the Negro hierarchy. SNCC works on the grassroots level and strives to let the people think, act, and decide for themselves. In reality, neither philosophy works purely, but there is a basic difference, which in Hermon's words makes it "absolutely impossible for SNCC and SCLC to work together." Apparently the SCLC dictatorship pattern prevailed in the Macon meeting on Saturday in which Hosea Williams, Martin Luther King's right-hand man, told the Negro "peon" what to do in a condescending manner. The result was that most of the people were alienated and angered by the conference (on voter registration).

It was very interesting to see the complete difference in approach when SCLC workers, Bill and Alfonso Harris, came in with Rev. Wells. They already had the answers and were going to move into the surrounding counties where SNCC was working and give the folks the word—voter registration.

Sherrod acted as a spokesman for the other view, since no SNCC workers were there. (Thank God. Think of the hell that would have broken loose!) Neither of the SCLC workers seemed as bright or as articulate as the SNCC workers. Nor did they have the SNCC style or jive talk, pride, and aggression. While they may be nicer guys, they don't command the respect of the SNCC workers.

It is obvious that a real political struggle is going on between the two groups. SNCC has the best philosophy, I think, but in southwest Georgia it has been unable to maintain enough discipline to carry its philosophy through. The thing the SNCC workers have the greatest reputation for is knocking up the local girls. Their approach is long and difficult and takes much perseverance. Few have the patience and the strength to stick with it. Charlie does and is extremely effective. I don't know about the others—except that none measures up to Charlie.

In its approach, SCLC has in its favor the long history of the Negro church, in which the preacher tells the folks what to do. Since most of the SCLC people are preachers, it makes it easier. Yet in following this approach, they seem to be perpetuating the age-old system, changing the "end" from salvation to "freedom." This brings the quickest results but ultimately will not bring the feeling of pride, of independence, growth, and freedom that I believe Sherrod's approach will bring. But things are so complex and intermingled, so that often in reality it depends on the individual person, who regardless of whether he is in SNCC or SCLC must do what he can. And individuals really aren't so different that they can't get together. There are bad workers and good workers in both groups. It is a shame that they must fight each other as much as they fight "Mister Charlie" [*slang for the white man*]. Yet it is also life.

After the mass meeting most of the young people went over to Pat Gaines's house for a party. There were probably around fifty people there, talking and dancing in the backyard. Hermon called a caucus of all the men to take up a collection to buy some wine. A hat was passed around and hands plunged into pockets. Before too long around four dollars was collected and off they went. The music played. Hot dogs were brought out. People danced and laughed. The wine was passed around. Everyone got about a third of a cupful. The hot dogs tasted good, roasted over an open charcoal grill. While the younger teenagers continued dancing, Eddie Brown, Hermon, Grady, Jo Ann, and Levita, and various other people, including almost all of the white volunteers, sat around the picnic table and sang. Wallace, Pfister, and Jim Perry gave a humorous rendition of the Grand Ole Opry (they know about ten times as much about it as I do), and we all sang spirituals and freedom songs. Mimy and I left around 1:00 and went back to the Meyerses'. During the course of the evening one of the SNCC workers hollered, "Hey, everybody—you Christians!—have some wine. It's communion!" Laughs followed. I thought a minute. Maybe he wasn't too far from the truth. . . .

June 14

This was a dismal and frustrating day. We slept late at the Meyerses' (9:00 a.m.), went by Mrs. Jackson's and gave her the information (or lack of it) from the Chamber of Commerce, then went to the SNCC office and waited for a call from the Baker County people. We stayed there all afternoon and did absolutely nothing except play several games of hearts. No call came.

The SNCC office is close to intolerable. People sit around all day, swearing, talking about smoking pot and sex, and hollering. After about thirty minutes, you must leave in order to keep your sanity.

At 6:00 p.m. Sherrod showed up and informed us that we were leaving in one hour for Baker, and we should pack all our bags. By 8:00 we had piled in two cars and were on our way. I had come down with something and felt a bit sick to my stomach, so my main concern was to get there without vomiting.

We reached the old castle-like church beyond Newton [*the Baker County seat*] at 9:30 p.m. and only one other car was there. A mass meeting had been supposed to start at 8:00 to kick off Josie Miller's campaign for the school board. By 9:45 about fifteen local people were present. Mrs. Holt chaired the meeting and talked about the problems with the Head Start program and how the whites would not let them use the grammar school. After that matter was kicked around, the failure to ascertain the registration fee for Mrs. Miller was brought up. Nothing was resolved in either case.

After an hour in the sticky heat, Rev. Wells got up and made a rousing speech for the local people to house us for the summer. Having thought Charlie had worked this out, we were rather ill at ease when the local people shrugged their shoulders. They had not expected we would be coming that night. Rev. Wells then ordered them all to leave the room and to make a decision. After they had left, he began to lecture to the young people about how bad the federal government was.

I was boiling inside. I detested Wells's strong-arm tactics, and I felt he and Charlie were forcing the local people to do something they weren't prepared to do. I exploded. It all came out on Charlie. I told him that this was no way to treat the local people and that the whole thing made me sick. He shrugged his shoulders and said that we should all talk about it.

Feaver had overheard all this and was infuriated at me for being unfair to Charlie by projecting all my pride and middle-class values onto a situation I did not understand. Ed was probably right—at any rate, I was not as mad at Charlie as I was at the whole frustrating mess. Here it was, 11:00 p.m. We were all exhausted and had no place to stay, and we still knew nothing of what we were to do or what we were there for. This seemed to me to be an outrage. The uncertainty of the summer, the disorganization and confusion. All of these things add up and build up.

Now we are beginning to see why it is so hard for people to change. Tearing away the old structures that give security—a yard, a home, family, a place to eat, a place to sleep, friends, a pattern of life. It is painful. We are feeling it ourselves. Not shaving or taking a bath eventually gets to you. And when you wonder why in the hell you are here, and no answer comes, it is hard to keep afloat.

After the meeting we drove back to Albany; and after a cup of coffee at Frank's [*the local dive near the SNCC office where we frequently ate*] we began to ponder again where we were to stay. (We had said our final goodbyes to the Meyerses.) Charlie came in and told us there were several places. Mimy and I ended up in Mrs. Webb's two-room apartment, very similar to the Meyerses'—no bath or hot water. She was sleeping in the kitchen on a lawn chair when we arrived around 12:30 a.m. and was expecting us. Later we found out that for some reason she had assumed we were not married and had told people that from now on no more unmarried couples were to stay with her. We later straightened the matter out and stayed there the next night, too.

June 15

We again awaited a call from Baker County that never came. The morning was hot and sticky, and after going to the River Road School at 8:30 only to find that there was not to be a lecture after all, and the Baker people weren't coming, we dismally wandered back to the SNCC office. Same old SNCC office. We did get to talk to Mrs. King, C. B.'s very articulate wife, who told us she wanted to talk to Sherrod and reach an understanding about our work. We emphasized that we were not to work on civil rights direct action so we probably would not end up being thrown in jail. She seemed to be concerned about our safety and appeared to be OK with this.

We met Charlie at Shiloh Baptist Church, where a meeting on voter registration began around 2:30. Wells led this meeting, dividing

Dougherty County into four parts. Charlie reported he had received thirty-two hundred dollars for the work and the canvassers would be paid twenty-five dollars a week.

After about an hour and a half, the meeting ended with vigorous singing. Of the twelve or so local people there, ten were high school girls (except Jo Ann), and they could really sing! "We Are Soldiers in the Army" lasted about fifteen minutes, with each of the girls taking leads.

At four o'clock the Baker County group met separately, and we kicked around what had happened the evening before. It was a good session. Various people aired their feelings and frustrations about the disorganization, chaotic living conditions, and the general uncertainty of the summer. Feaver maintained that the ripping away of structure was basically good and could be creative. It was absolutely necessary that we face ourselves and come through it, if we had any ideas about effecting change or ministering.

The meeting came at a low point in the summer thus far for me and Ed's speech gave us new life. For the first time in several days I felt that we might possibly become a group after all.

Toward the close of the meeting, Mickey and Larry [*the other couple that summer—everyone else was single*] announced that they were to be "Mr. and Mrs." from now on. This necessitated an official wedding ceremony, which the Rev. Sherrod performed with true Sherrod creativity. Holding each other's little fingers in a circle, we awaited the spirit to unite us and form the perfect whole. When everyone's eyes were shut, the spirit moved in its mysterious way and united the gap between Mickey and Larry, making them man and wife.

The whole event was hilarious and helped relieve a lot of the tension. We all went to Charlie's friend's house for a huge fried chicken dinner, after which Mimy and I took a much needed shower at Ed and Joe's pad. At 8:00, we all went bowling.

June 16

Today we departed for Baker County, this time to stay. In the morning, we went to the Head Start training session and spent over an hour with Mrs. C. B. King, who showed us one of the Albany centers. The most impressive thing is that the programs really are integrated. Whites and Negroes work alongside each other happily and peacefully;

and black and white children play together. Supposedly the teaching staff is 50 percent white, and there are a large number of white children in the program. Without the marches, sit-ins, and boycotts, this never would have happened; but it is happening now and it is certainly one of the fruits of the movement. Ironically (or naturally!), SNCC workers scoff at it, saying the people in it are sell-outs to the federal government. While SNCC can break things open, it cannot pick up the pieces and put things together again. This is what is happening in Head Start in Albany. It is small, but it is an exciting and impressive start.

In the afternoon, after finally getting things lined up, five of us (Chris, Mickey, Larry, Mimy, and I) departed for Baker. Ellen had opted for voter registration work in Albany.

We got to East Baker High School around 3:30, just in time to find out who we were to live with. Mimy and I were assigned to the Holts. Mrs. Holt is the head cook for Head Start and one of the leaders in the movement. Her husband is a sixty-five-year-old farmer who has lived his entire life on their 280-acre farm, which he now shares with his brother-in-law. They have two boys, Jackie, seventeen, and Nathaniel, usually called Nathan (pronounced with both syllables getting the same emphasis), twelve.

The house is sort of run down and dirty, three bedrooms, and no water inside, no plumbing whatsoever. It is going to be somewhat of an adjustment getting used to living here—the bugs, flies, lack of toilet facilities. But Mimy and I have our own bedroom and the countryside is beautiful.

The Holts are all very nice. Mrs. Holt is buxom, talkative, and full of love. Mr. Holt is slow and quiet and is first and foremost a farmer. This was his daddy's farm before his, and he is proud of it. For a sixty-five-year-old man, he really gets around. He does almost all the work himself and looks about forty-five! [*Not sure why it was not mentioned here but Mr. Holt was partially blind and totally lost his sight a few years later.*] The boys I like, too. Jackie is going through teenage rebellion, hanging out with "the guys" and trying to look cool. (Though he fails. He's too nice to look cool.)

The family is a mixture of the old and the new. Mr. and Mrs. Holt are deeply religious. Someone goes to church just about every night, and they really love the church and God. Mrs. Holt is similarly caught up in the movement, which may now be playing a role much like the church (giving community and meaning). Jackie is of the new breed, not too interested in farming, though he still goes to church.

Mimy and I are in a new situation. There is so much to learn. The challenges are great.

June 17–18

These were days in which I experienced what might be called "culture shock." I had a throbbing headache both days. I am realizing how difficult it is to transition from one culture to another. I can accept the change rationally, but emotionally is another thing. The eating habits, toilet habits, language, etc., are as different as being in Mexico or Japan. Over the past two days my senses have been dulled, and my chief concern has been survival. Consequently, much has happened that I have been unable to perceive or respond to.

What really makes the situation difficult is the pressure I am beginning to feel from Charlie and the SNCC group and my own ego "to *do* something," and the realization that I am really out of it and can't do *anything*. This, combined with the awareness that the whites are hostile to us and that we are not completely safe, makes it very hard for me to feel at ease in the present situation. This "culture shock" has manifested itself in a feeling of listlessness and the ringing headache.

Mimy has held up extremely well—though she is feeling the same pressures as I am. What makes it bearable for both of us is that we can take walks in the fields and talk about it all to each other. She has been a great help to me, especially in the past two days. We will make it, but it is extremely hard.

This is where we really need strength that we don't have. Will this strength come from God? If I ever needed God, if I ever wanted faith, I need it now.

God have mercy on us.

Give us strength.

Help us to love when there is no love in us.

Help us to walk when our legs are crumbling beneath us.

Help us to give when we feel as if we have nothing.

Help us to be ourselves when we don't even know who we are.

Amen.

June 19

[*This was our first Sunday in Baker County, an experience I still remember vividly, forty years later.*]

It has been a busy day. In the back of the Holts' old truck, we rode to the church, an old white frame building just up the road. Although we were a half-hour late for Sunday school, only three people were present when we arrived. One by one people drifted in. By noon when the service was to begin, about thirty were present; and before it was over at 2:00, there must have been about seventy.

The service was amazing. Most of the prayers were sung, with the responses sung, wailed, and moaned. Many of the songs seemed to be like what slave chants might have sounded like [*these were beautiful call-and-response spirituals*]. Many of the prayers focused on bearing a yoke and being in bondage with the hope of one day being "free with Jesus." The preacher, an elderly, bald "shouter," capitalized on the slavery motif but made no connection with civil rights. It is amazing how in the nonmovement meetings, all talk of civil rights is avoided. His sermon was wild at times and hard to follow. His two main points were how war is wrong and how prayers are good, but rather than explain or elaborate on the themes, he shouted formulas and, by chanting and even singing, built up the desired emotions to get over thirty dollars in three offerings.

Much of the service was beautiful. The spontaneity and the freedom of the worshippers, the lively singing, the deep feelings, the chanting and responsiveness. Some was disappointing—the paternalism of the pastor, the docility and credulousness of the congregation. Because the preacher said it—it was right. But this is not entirely the case, for when the preacher is not preaching, he can be questioned. It is the *role* of the preacher that seems to be sacrosanct. And this preacher was fairly emotional but not a movement man, by any means. "Just remember," he said, "since these white folks are here we got to be on our number one behavior—but you got to stay in your place!" This was really embarrassing to me.

The people were very friendly toward us and gave us a very warm welcome. I made a brief introduction and was asked by the preacher—when Mrs. Holt told him I was a "minister student"—to help him preach. I refused.

At 2:30, Sherrod and Wells picked us up for another service at Thankful Church. Very similar. At 5:00, we went to a Head Start meeting at the high school. At 8:00, the mass meeting. Good attendance, good spirit. Mr. Philip Bailey agreed to run for the Board of Education. Chuck Lawrence [*my brother D. G.'s friend from Yale Law School*] presented a plan to get Negroes on jury lists and a plan to get rid of Sheriff Johnson. Several agreed to work on the jury plan. No one wanted to mess with the sheriff. People aren't over all of their fears by a long shot. Most of the meeting was spent on the campaign—a special meeting was set for Friday. A great meeting—a good feeling. Things are beginning to move. A good day. For the first time, we are beginning to feel a part of things.

June 20

The first day of Head Start. The children began arriving shortly after 8:00; and by 8:30 there were wide-eyed gaping little boys and girls all over the place. A few cried, a few seemed unhappy the whole time, but they were as a whole surprisingly well behaved, happy, and easy to entertain. Only seventy-two of the 110 expected showed up, so we had only twelve in our room. Most of the time they rolled the spools, played with the kitchen stuff, and rode the tractor. [*The play equipment was improvised.*] Even with the drastic shortage of material, the day went extremely smoothly.

The new education director, Miss Ann Runk, seems very sharp and should help the program greatly. [*Ann Runk, who was white, was an extremely experienced early childhood educator from the Bank Street School in New York City. She came for the summer to run Head Start and lived just down the street from the Holts, with the Broadways. We became good friends over the summer, although we lost touch afterward.*]

After Head Start, we went to Albany with Isaac, who was here to try to find another candidate for the Board of Education. Bailey withdrew for unknown reasons. (It is interesting that the Hawkins fellow, the "Tom," was at the mass meeting yesterday and had a private meeting with him!) The meeting finally got under way around 5:00 at Jo Ann Christian's. Reports were passed around. People told of their work.

My concern now is fear of being pressured and pressed. There is so much we are supposed to be doing—the credit union, ASCS elections, get-rid-of-Johnson, jury lists, welfare rolls, student center, the Board of Education campaign, etc. All this on top of Head Start—which is itself a real challenge. Sherrod keeps pushing, saying we've got to work all the time—there's no such thing as a holiday, etc. People make long reports of how the movement is really going somewhere, under their indirect leadership. I am wondering how much is real and how much is self-serving.

And what are *we* doing? *We* are managing to survive. That is about it. We are listening and trying to get to know the people. We are trying just to be ourselves. Why is this so damn hard? How can we begin to do all the other stuff? Sometimes it feels like a vise were closing in—all this plus the realization that if we ever really were to do any of this other stuff, it could be very dangerous.

We got a ride back with McInroy and spent a long time chatting with the Holts. A lot came out about the origins of the movement. Another long day.

June 21

Head Start went very well. Mimy and I left with the bus at 2:30 and rode with the kids through a countryside straight out of *Gone with the Wind*: Blacky's, Pineland, Tarva, Blue Springs, and Itchuaway. [*These are the names of the Baker County plantations, where the children we taught lived in small cabins, and where their parents were sharecroppers or farm laborers.*] I had once thought that "plantations" were Georgia's way of saying "large farms." I was wrong. These are real plantations. Acres and acres of deep green pastures, crops, woods, lakes, and swamps. Rows of servants' quarters, huge barns, race tracks, Big Houses. It's all out of the storybooks.

The bus rattled down narrow, winding roads, letting the kids off one by one. After about an hour and a half we were in Pineland. Just as we had passed the magnificent Big House the bus stopped; there it remained for two hours and forty-five minutes and still remains. [*The plantation was owned by the Mellon family, which founded the National Gallery in Washington, and was used primarily for hunting, though substantial crops were grown on the land.*] Something went wrong with the wiring system, and Mr. Jackson was unable to fix it. So Mimy and I had to handle about forty squirming, restless five- and six-year-olds on their second day of school. At 6:30 p.m. Mr. Jackson managed to return with another bus, which broke down about fifty yards from our first bus. Finally, it was fixed and we got going, only to break down again in front of the

Newton courthouse! Mimy and I rode the whole route and got back to the Holts' around 9:00 p.m.

All in all, it was a tiring experience, but it was not a tragedy. We sang songs and played games and generally kept spirits from falling too low. The children were amazingly well behaved and patient. A few cried and a few got into fights, and everyone was pretty miserable before we got home, but everyone held up very, very well. Mimy and I just happened to go with them this afternoon. Had we not decided to go for the "sightseeing tour," only one adult would have been with the kids. The Holy Spirit was working.

June 23

Headache and depression return. I'm not sure why I have been so depressed. Perhaps it's because I'm still not sure what I (we) are doing here. I'm not sure where we fit in or where we can really be of help. I'm afraid of the possibility of death, and I feel that the possibility is real. We have hardly seen a white man, let alone been threatened. Nevertheless, today the thought of death has been real and has really bothered me.

Also I feel threatened by some of the other volunteers. I feel that Charlie expects us to be doing more than we are either willing or able to do. I feel the other civil rights workers resent us because of our "safe" and routine work at Head Start. Obviously I'm projecting many of my own feelings of inferiority onto the situation, but the feelings are real.

What is the movement all about? Do I have the guts to give my *life* to it? What am I doing here?

At times I long for a safe, secure home in suburbia. So much in the movement is confused, mixed up, and ugly. I understand why it is so difficult for people to change. Mimy adjusts amazingly well, and much better than I. I admire her but sometimes feel alienated from her. She tends to shut herself off in her own little world and we do not always really communicate. I do the same thing and am equally at fault.

I wish I were on top of things. I wish I could say exactly why we are here. I wish I could say I am not afraid. I wish I could say I could really help these people.

I am learning. But the learning is very painful. I don't know why it should be this way. Nothing spectacular has happened. Thank God! Nothing to brag about or even write home about. We are simply living with a wonderful Negro family, a family much wiser, braver, and more mature than we are, or probably ever will be. This can be said about so many others, Mrs. Josie Miller, Mrs. Grace Miller, whose husband was shot in cold blood by a white man spring before last, and many, many others we don't yet know.

June 24

The first day in several days I have lasted until dinner without a headache. The first week of Head Start is past. Tomorrow we are going to Quitman. [*My grandmother, Louise Lott McMichael, lived in Quitman, Georgia, in Brooks County, not one of the counties covered by the Southwest Georgia Project, but very nearby. It so happened that at that time she was in the hospital, and we went for the weekend to visit her.*]

Yesterday after Head Start, Chris came over to inform us that Isaac had invited us to Hermon's birthday party. Isaac picked us up at 7:30 and we had a good talk on the way in. He talked of all the previous activity in Baker, especially with Sheriff Johnson. He was more open than I had ever seen him.

The party for Hermon was small and for us quite unusual. Beer, wine, gin, and moonshine. Wild jazz. Dark, and *pot!* [*Smoking marijuana was not yet so common on college campuses at that time.*]

There were five whites (us, Ellen, Chris, and Charles Wallace) and several SNCC guys who were quite open and friendly. The more I know these guys the more I respect them, especially Isaac and Hermon, who is leaving in a couple of weeks for a ten-thousand-dollar-a-year job in the antipoverty program. He said he knew he was a sellout and a "phony," but he needed "the bread." Eddie was in rare form: sunglasses, undershirt, and high on pot. They passed the stuff around for us to smoke, but no one except me took any, and I didn't inhale. As for the effect it had on the SNCC guys, I really didn't notice any difference in their behavior. Isaac stayed sober so he could drive us back. Damn thoughtful of him. Underneath all the show, these people are warm, sensitive human beings.

Hermon's choice comment of the evening: "Hell, the poverty job is a big joke. It's just like SNCC except you get paid ten thousand dollars. You sit around and goof off half the time."

The funniest thing was when Eddie tried to convince three local people that we were going to have a meeting and they had to leave. Only

Eddie and I were in the room with the men, and there was laughter and music coming from inside. Obviously a party going on. Eddie went over to them and said, "OK, let's start the meeting. Somebody take notes. This is very important. Meeting come to order. Err, excuse me. But we are starting now. Will you guys please, you know. . . ." They got the point and shuffled out of the room.

Today was easier. Slowly we are beginning to find a place. Our role is not to be great civil rights workers but human beings, teaching in Head Start and living and being with the people. It takes time to be with the people, but slowly that is coming. We don't have answers. We're no great heroes. We are just one of them for the summer. It's not spectacular, but it is the best role we could possibly be in. We don't have to play the big act or do or say things we don't know anything about. We can just be ourselves and be with them. They are good people. We have much to learn from them.

June 26

Back from Quitman where we saw Mama and Munny, who is recovering from a heart attack. [*This is my mother and grandmother. I suppose at this time he was still using the nickname for my mother that her children used. At some point not long thereafter, she asked him to use Louise, and they became great friends. I did not remember that she was in Quitman for this visit, but I do remember seeing my grandmother in the hospital and her increasing awareness of what we were doing, of which I believe she secretly approved.*] We saw lots of relatives, cousins, and friends, and without too much effort avoided almost all talk of our activity. It was an extremely tedious experience, and I felt uneasy most of the time; but all of it was very good. Driving to Thomasville, we had a very good talk with Mrs. McMichael [*I believe this would be Laura McMichael, my mother's first cousin*], who is trying hard to grow with regard to civil rights issues. But the gap seems so great. She wants to do the right thing, but everything she says reeks with paternalism. Nevertheless, in spite of her talk about the "Nigras," she is trying and I respect her. She did not seem to resent us for what we are doing and gave us the name of a white person to contact in Camilla [*a town within the Southwest Georgia Project area*]. She said to stay away from the Newton people.

The whole situation seems so sad. There is a great deal of love between the races. But there is so little real understanding, so much fear of meeting the Negro on his level. We are in a unique situation in being able to pass from one community to the other. But it is not easy. We are really not a part of either community, and it gives us a strange, uneasy feeling.

After a bus ride to Camilla, the Fosters picked us up and drove us to the Holts'. It was good to see our "Mama and Daddy." [*By this time we truly felt adopted by this warm, wonderful family.*] Mrs. Holt is so amazing: "Christians and non-Christians are like sheep and hogs. The sheeps fall in the mud, but they get up. The hog falls in and wallows. Christians are like babes in Christ. You got to grow. Put God ahead of everything. He'll put words in your mouth. Have faith." She has this faith, and God is present in her. "Pray for guidance and understanding and strength. He'll give it to you." Thanks be to God for Mrs. Holt.

Tonight there was a mass meeting; about sixty people were there. Sherrod reported on violence in Cordele and threats of violence in Worth, after which he and Wells left. The meeting went very well without them. There are so many strong people in Baker—Richard Wright, the young (about thirty) dog trainer from Ichauway, Mr. Julius Williams, Mr. Broadway, Mr. Cowart, etc. The spirit was higher than the past few meetings. Mrs. Josie [*Miller*]'s husband, Walter, was drunk as usual and made an unfortunate spectacle of himself. There was general negative reaction to him, with many people walking out while he talked.

Mr. Cowart made an impressive acceptance comment, saying he would not be bought off by the "Caucasian race." [*Davie Cowart was the person who eventually ran for Board of Education that summer.*] The meeting went a little slower, but I felt it went much better without Charlie and Rev. Wells. More people expressed themselves and expressed themselves very well. It was a good feeling to be there. We are feeling more and more a part of the community.

June 30

So far this week has been fairly typical. Monday was another staff meeting, held in the SNCC office in Albany. Ellen reported on the violence in Cordele in her typical unintelligible jive fashion. She did convey a situation of chaos and turmoil and hostile feelings toward "SNCC spokesman" Bill Konnover. Other reports followed—Feaver, Pfister, and Romberg have been threatened practically every day in Worth County working on voter registration. The voter drive is continuing in Albany. After the meeting, the bowling group headed for the alleys. . . .

Tuesday was a hard, hot day at Head Start. The children are becoming more and more rambunctious and the teachers more and more passive. Personalities are becoming clearer, and problems are evident in many of them. The hot suffocating weather doesn't help matters. [*Of course there was no air conditioning anywhere that summer, and this was the Deep South.*] Tuesday afternoon we went "swimming" at the Broadways', taking a cool shower under the hose.

Wednesday was another hard day at Head Start, but the situation is generally good and we are on top of it. That evening, we drove into Newton for the meeting of the Georgia Council on Human Relations, held in the courthouse. Of the fifty people there, about half were Negroes from Baker. The others included Negroes from Thomasville, Sylvester, and a few other communities. A considerable number came down from Atlanta, including Mrs. Pawley, the beloved director, a very homey, elderly white person; with her was an Episcopal minister and a Negro chairman. There were probably about fifteen white people, all of them either in our group or on the Atlanta staff. Just after the meeting had begun, three rough-looking white men wandered in and sat in the jury section so they could see everyone. They just sat there and stared the whole evening, and later they were joined by several other rough-looking characters and some teenagers who wandered in and out. One of the men we later learned was the murderer of Mr. Miller.

The meeting began with singing. The bald-headed Episcopal minister was leading "Jacob's Ladder" [*the spiritual*] when Mr. Holt and I entered the room. The singing was good old south Georgia style with deep emotion and feeling. Mr. Holt and Mrs. Grace Miller [*whose husband's murderer was observing the proceedings*] alternated leads, concluding with "We Shall Overcome."

The first speaker was an elderly southern white man who was the head of a state program that had to do with establishing credit unions. He talked for about thirty minutes and covered the main points in a colorful, southern, incoherent rambling fashion. There was mild response from the people. After a few questions, the first man and his assistant left. Then a young middle-class person in his late twenties got up and nervously went over the same material using cards. He must have been a college football player, since he looked to me like a Fellowship of Christian Athletes hero. He was clearer than the first man, and the response was a little better.

Then a man from the ASCS spoke on the new election rulings. He said that many candidates must be placed on the ASCS ballot to equal the percentage of Negroes in the county. In other words, in Baker more than half the candidates must be Negro! Also, any farmer can nominate new names for the ballot if this is done twenty-five days before the election, which this year will be September 23. This is a real breakthrough, if the Baker people will only take advantage of it.

The man's name was Wasserman, and he also represented the National Sharecroppers' Union. I could almost hear sizzling coming from inside the three "crackers" sitting in the jury section. Wasserman also talked of opportunities in the antipoverty program for industry, jobs, roads, etc. White supremacy is slowly on its way out in Baker. But it is still going to be a long, long time.

The meeting was a very good experience. A lot of good solid things were said about credit unions, ASCS, and antipoverty programs. For the first time in history, an integrated group assembled for a meeting in the courthouse. There was not much time for socializing and refreshments were not offered, but a good spirit prevailed, and people went away beaming.

July 1

There was another special mass meeting at Thankful Church Thursday evening, but only about fifteen local people were present, and no one from Albany showed up. As a result, not much was accomplished. Mrs. Holt and Mrs. Miller said they would canvas the county this weekend, but two people can go only so far. This being the first time these people have ever been involved in an election, it is easy to understand why there are difficulties. They have little idea of how to even *begin* a campaign, and they need help urgently. But neither Isaac, Charlie, nor Wells were there. I spent some time that evening talking with Mrs. Holt, but it was difficult to really communicate. I suggested she try to get other people to help her and Mrs. Miller canvass and to designate responsibility to others. She listened and said that this was a good idea, but I don't think she is prepared or able to do this. As of now, things have remained about the same, and any formal campaign or organization is nonexistent. I have tried to suggest certain things to her and Mrs. Miller, but realize I can go only so far. [*Because of the deal Sherrod brokered allowing us to work in Baker, namely, that white people would not take a visible lead in direct civil rights organizing there.*] I think I have said enough. There is real need for Charlie and Isaac now. How extremely difficult it is to try to organize a community! How far away these people are from the SNCC mentality of political organization!

July 2

It's Saturday. Up at 8:45. It's a bright, clear day with hot sun and cool shadows. Breakfast of grits and fried fish and cornbread. Mrs. Holt gets ready to go to town with Mrs. Foster. Jackie mows the pasture. Mr. Holt and Mr. Broadway go to Camilla to pick up the hogsheads. [*This was in preparation for a big Fourth of July feast.*] Everyone takes his time. Mimy and I sit on the front porch in the shadows and shell butter beans. Before too long Mrs. Foster arrives—about an hour behind schedule. Mr. Holt returns after a while and sits on the porch with us, and we begin to chat. He talks of fishing and snakes and hunting alligators. He talks in a slow, deep drawl, and what he says sounds like poetry. There is a rich, lyrical quality in his speech that is mystifying. If only there were a tape recorder!

A little while later, Isaac and Mrs. Josie drive up in the SNCC car, decorated with posters of Mr. Cowart.

Isaac asks me if I want to go and I grab my camera and hop in. We drive over winding, sandy roads, stopping at one farmhouse after another. Mrs. Josie does most of the talking. "Jest doin' a little campaigning. You know we got a colored candidate, Davie Cowart, Saul Cowart's son . . ."

"Oh yeah, I know," a white-haired woman replies. "You don't have to tell *me* to vote for him. I dun made up my mind about that. It's about time for a change. White folks haint dun nothin' for us. It's our time to give it a try." The talk continues, the weather, the farm, neighbors, Mr. Cowart.

The countryside is beautiful. The farms are usually small. Many of the houses are shacks. We drive through Ichauway [*huge plantation owned by the Woodruff family of Coca-Cola fame*]. The road winds through rich green fields. Talking, talking, talking. Good responses. Everyone says they'll vote for Cowart.

Back home by way of Grace Miller's, Jackie and Bobby Broadway are there canvassing.

We talk to Mr. Holt for about an hour, sitting on the porch. Nathan and I toss the Frisbee. Mrs. Holt returns, and we have dinner at 9:00. After dinner we sit and rock on the porch. Mr. Holt begins to weave threads and pieces of the past. We listen, amazed by his memory of details and his rich style.

Gunsmoke is on [*although the Holts did not have indoor plumbing, they had electricity and a TV*]. We go in at 10:30. Eleven o'clock and we turn in. It has been a good day.

July 3

We sit on the porch, rock, and listen to Mr. Holt tell about his grandmother who was in slavery. He tells how she told him of her ride over in a ship, which was almost capsized by a whale. At Charleston, she "married" a man who was later sold to a family in Georgia named Holt. They were later sold to a man named Hanes who, when the Civil War was over, sold to his grandfather the plot of land they live on now.

He tells of the Great Depression, of lynchings, and of murders of Negroes. It is hard to follow his complicated narrative. There are so many fascinating details.

At 11:30, Nathan is ordered off to Sunday school, which supposedly began an hour before. Mrs. Holt is feeling bad. Mr. Holt rides up to Carl's. Nathan returns at 11:45 saying that he and his five cousins were "a little late." We throw the Frisbee. Mimy and I take a hose bath in the back pasture. It is great to be alive.

In the afternoon, we walked over to the Broadways', where all the relatives were beginning to arrive. There we met Jennie, Ann, and Chris, and walked with them and several of Nathan's friends to the old "haunted house" down the road [*"hunted house" in Mr. Holt's drawl*]. Many in the Holt family had lived there at one time or another, but now the house is in shambles. Overgrown with flowers, bushes, vines, and Spanish moss, it is intriguing, as all haunted houses should be. Across from it and down the road a bit is an old graveyard that has been entirely obscured by the moss and foliage. The graveyard lies on the edge of a large swampy pond, with all kinds of wildlife, including eels and alligators. The road leads into the swamp. Many years ago, before the swamp existed, the road had gone all the way to Newton. How long ago that was may be mythical, for Mrs. Holt says the swamp has been there for a hundred years. At any rate, now the road dead ends in a bog. There the moss hangs from the trees in dangling thick heaps; and in the late afternoon when the sun floods the thick foliage, a very eerie effect is created. It is one of the most beautiful sights I have ever seen.

We walked down to the pond and then back along the road, picking blackberries and fresh plums as we walked. We returned to the Holts' around 7:00 and ate watermelon. Ed, Joe, and Jim showed up looking for the barbecue, which Charlie had told them was to be that day. They went back hungry. They told us that the songfest had come off pretty well and that things had gone OK at the Cordele "swim-in." One hundred and twenty troopers were there, but someone had let all the water out of the pool. [*The swim-in was an effort to desegregate the Cordele public pool. Blacks would show up at a white-only pool and jump in, usually resulting in their arrests. I am not sure what Joe meant here when he said things went well, except possibly that there were no arrests and no one got hurt.*]

The mass meeting was that evening. Only a handful of local people were there—perhaps thirty—and there must have been at least as many outsiders—people from Cordele, Albany, and many SNCC and SCLC workers. Wells and Sherrod made their entrance midway through the meeting and proceeded to take over the show. The more Wells talks, the more he appears to me a pompous demagogue who really does not understand the people.

Not much was accomplished at the meeting. The people need organizational help. They need someone who will work more and talk less. They need to work more and talk less themselves. They do not need to be harangued at and talked down to!

That evening when we returned Mr. Holt and Mr. Broadway, and others, were cooking the two-and-a-half pigs over the coals. It was a beautiful evening, warm with a full moon. The old folks were sitting around chatting, and the men were so proud of those pigs. They were still talking when we turned in after midnight and I understand stayed up all night.

I took several of the youngsters up to the haunted house—no ghosts appeared.

July 4

The Fourth was gay, with all the out-of-town relatives and a delicious barbecue.

[*I am amazed that this is the extent of Joe's entry about the Fourth of July, because—while most of the details of events he lays out in this diary have faded into oblivion for me forty years later, the Fourth of July barbecue is still vivid in my mind. More than twenty-five relatives of the Holts and Broadways arrived, having driven from all over the country to "come home" for the Fourth. The night before the men dug a very deep pit and laid a big fire. Once it died down, they sat up all night talking and basting the roasting pigs and a goat. (Although pigs were common food—bacon and lard especially—the goat meat seemed to be a special thing for the Fourth.) The hogsheads mentioned earlier were used the next day to make an enormous Brunswick stew with lots of fresh vegetables from the garden such as corn, tomatoes, okra, etc. Of course, there were fried chicken, biscuits, cakes, watermelon, and many other good things to eat, along with the best barbecue I've ever tasted. The closeness that this dispersed clan felt to their roots there in southwest Georgia was very evident and very moving. Now when they have the large "Black Family Reunion" on the National Mall in Washington every year, I understand well the type of event it is based on.*]

July 8

This past week has been slow and leisurely. Between the hot, sweaty mornings of screaming children and the preparations for Mr. Cowart's election, there have been lazy afternoons with long walks to the haunted house and the swamp, and hose baths in the Broadways' backyard. Our relationship with Ann and Jean has grown, and we have come to like and respect them very much. [*Jean was also an early childhood educator, a black woman from somewhere outside southwest Georgia. She lived at the Broadways' with Ann for the summer.*]

Head Start has been exhausting, but it is very rewarding. Many of the children are growing and responding extremely well. There have been problems. Many of the aides [*local people hired as assistant teachers like us*] have not been giving the children proper attention, but generally the program has gone very well. Ann is a great director. Without her leadership, I don't know where we would be. She is especially warm and sensitive with the children and a great example for us to follow. She is the youngest thirty-eight-year-old woman I have ever seen. [*Of course to us, in our early twenties, thirty-eight years old was OLD!*]

The campaign for Mr. Cowart got under way this week, but excitement was minimal, and even less was done. Mrs. Miller and Mrs. Holt talk a lot but don't do a great deal. Organizational help is needed. I have tried to suggest and encourage but have not gotten much response. Isaac came by Wednesday and helped get Bobby Broadway and friends moving. I went along to be sure they got past the Millers. (Last week they spent the whole afternoon there.) Since Bobby's car had no reverse gear and a weak coil—and every time the motor stopped it needed a push-off—our progress was rather sporadic. We managed to cover the Anna district, canvassing over fifteen houses, and broke down only twice. The second time occurred beside a cotton field, where a group of fifteen (perhaps two families of women and children, and one man) were hoeing cotton. The same scene could have occurred two hundred years ago. Three of the teenagers hiked down the road and found an old Negro man with a 1949 Pontiac and jump wires.

The response to the canvassing was not as positive as the previous day, when Isaac, Mrs. Josie, and I covered El Model [*a settlement a few miles from Newton*]. That day everyone knew of the election and was for it all the way. With the teenagers, several people did not even know of the election and many weren't registered to vote. Anna is in the farthest part of the county from Newton.

The week has been a good one. I have had a deep sense of satisfaction, more so than I can remember for a long time. Mimy and I love the people and the country here so much. The Holts are so great. The scenery is rejuvenating. This week I have felt freer and happier than at any time since I was at Union [*so over a two-year period*]. Mimy and I would love to live in such a community and devote our lives to helping the community grow in spirit. This summer the reverse is happening— they are helping us grow in spirit.

Ashley [*Wiltshire*] arrived yesterday and will be staying at the Holts' the remainder of the summer as our new "brother." [*He shared a room with the Holt boys.*] We will have less "free" time, but he is a good person and we are glad he is here. [*Ashley was a fellow seminary student, also from the South (Virginia), who for some reason arrived later in the summer than the rest of us, and who became a close friend over the summer. He was a liberal Southern Baptist who could not stomach the direction his church was taking (in terms of civil rights and social issues), so he eventually went to law school. He later became head of the Legal Aid Society of Nashville and Middle Tennessee, where he worked his entire career.*]

130

July 9

This weekend was the notorious trip to Jekyll Island. [*Jekyll Island is a very fancy resort on the Georgia coast, which up until this time had not been integrated.*] It all began with my suggestion to Charlie that since so many people from Baker County wanted to go to the beach for the meeting of the Georgia Council on Human Relations [*one of the few racially integrated groups in the state, based in Atlanta*], we should all go down there for the weekend. Charlie agreed and set the departure time for 4:00 a.m. from Albany. Despite several phone calls to protest leaving at such an early hour, we were forced to comply.

We got up at 3:00 a.m. and left the Holts' at 4:00 a.m. Since the truck wouldn't start, we had to call the Broadways for help. After more confusion, we finally got off from the school at 4:30, with six of the original eighteen showing up.

When we reached Albany at 5:30 a.m., the rest of the group was there and ready to go. We all piled into the Sherrod bus, riding three per seat, and rode the long route to the sea, making three stops, one at Sylvester, one by a policeman, and one gas stop. The trooper kept us for thirty minutes, maintaining we did not have the right tags. We must have really terrified white folks in the little country store when black and white together we piled out of the bus.

Upon reaching Jekyll Island at 11:00 a.m., we went to the Georgia Council meeting. They were overjoyed to have us. We certainly *looked* like "poor people," and being a middle-class group, they needed to reach "poor people." Most of the sixty or seventy delegates were nicely dressed in coats and ties. Our group had on everything from overalls, Levis, sandals, and sweatshirts; and we had long hair and beards, the works. The contrast became increasingly humorous as the weekend went on. The "Sherrod group" was about fifty or so and included SIM and SNCC workers, as well as a handful of local people from the counties. We began to take over the motel. Without paying a cent, we went swimming in the pools, used motel facilities for dressing, used their beach, and had a free meal. That evening eighteen of us slept on the motel beach. Under any other circumstances, I am sure we would have been kicked out or arrested within fifteen minutes of arrival. Yet, because the Georgia Council had set the conference up, and because we were "poor people" and therefore good for the middle-class folks to have around, there was not very much that could be done. Much that our group did struck me as offensive—crashing the

131

teenage party, marauding around the beach like an army of guerrillas, generally disturbing the peace by singing freedom songs, and hollering. The jive talk and the "civil rights creeps" [*Joe: This was one of Ashley's many colorful descriptive terms along with "Trunk Cases" and "Freenballs." Ashley had a way of getting to the bottom line and sizing people up quickly and accurately.*] were also irritating at times, but the motel people were surprisingly tolerant.

That evening we all sneaked onto the beach. Since Mimy and I had only one thin blanket, we were eaten alive by mosquitoes and got a little chilly. I got about two hours of sleep and spent the rest of the time slapping insects. We got up at 5:00 and walked along the beach. It was worth it to see the sunrise.

That weekend we got a good mental and emotional rest, if not a physical one. It was good for all of us to get together for a leisurely meeting. The only real misfortune was that Mimy lost a contact lens. The motel people will recover, though I doubt if the Georgia Council will be allowed back!

July 12

Tomorrow is the election. Wells, Isaac, and the "SNCC cats" came out and as usual did not do very much. There was an argument between Charlie, who wanted outsiders to come in and help with transportation, and Isaac, who insisted the local people should carry the load. Ashley and I expressed Mrs. Holt's and Mrs. Williams's feelings that outsiders would only bring trouble. If a group of outsiders do come in, it will be waving a red flag in front of the crackers. If this election goes smoothly—even if Mr. Cowart is defeated—it should dispel many of the fears Negroes have. If there is violence, it will reinforce these fears and create many more. It is very important that we do not irritate the whites to the extent that they retaliate with more violence, especially when there is no reason for irritating them.

It is very easy to see how violence occurs, simply because of irresponsibility and egotism on the part of the civil rights workers.

It has been an unusual "campaign." No organization in any formal sense, no systematic canvassing of the community, not much enthusiasm on the part of anyone. Yet the word is apparently out. There is no telling what is going to happen. Supposedly transportation of voters is set up, but again things are not as organized as I would like for them to be. Here I am, imposing a middle-class bias on all of this—in so many ways the casual, slow-moving pace is idyllic. There is something very beautiful about the life here that we will miss very, very much.

I don't think Cowart has much of a chance, but who knows? Maybe there will be a real upset. Since two whites are still in the race, there is at least a good possibility of a runoff. Tomorrow we shall see.

We have just returned from the second night of revival week at St. Matthew's Church. In many ways it was very depressing. Rev. Pinkney is a horrible preacher! He shouts, jumps, and screams and makes no sense whatsoever. People respond by saying "yes, sir" and "A-men" to the nonsense phrases. The preacher is the authority and whatever he says is God's word, even if it happens to be gibberish. The Negro church it seems to me is very much a part of the old system of white paternalism and slavery. The sermons dwell on sin and inferiority and pie-in-the-sky salvation. The preacher is above it all and preaches down to the servile congregation. How much longer can such a church last? With more and more people beginning to feel some degree of independence and self-worth and with the growing rebellion against paternalism, I do not think this church as it stands now will survive. The old form must be especially disagreeable to the young folks. I wonder how intelligent, perceptive people like Mrs. Holt and Mrs. Josie can tolerate it. Yet they do not utter one word of criticism against the church. The miracle is that *in spite of* the church, they live a life which embodies the Christian spirit—humility, love, and strength. And they are the first to give all credit to God. It is a very amazing situation.

The humorous aspect of the meeting was that "Reverend Irish Potato" (Ashley) [*Mrs. Holt could not pronounce "Reverend Ashley Wiltshire" and it came out "Reverend Irish Potato" (what they called white potatoes) and the nickname stuck*] was the assistant preacher. He is officially "Reverend Irishley" or "Irish" and will probably be saving souls before long. [*Joe: Ashley was actually an excellent preacher and had no qualms about preaching, as I did.*]

July 14

Yesterday Davie Cowart polled 349 votes. Cecil Mulford, Sheriff Johnson's man, got 604, and the third man polled only 193. Mulford won it without a runoff.

There are almost seven hundred registered Negroes and fourteen hundred registered whites. Apparently around four hundred Negroes voted.

It was neither a bad nor a good showing. It was generally as expected. Half the registered Negroes voted, and almost all of them voted for Cowart. With more work in future campaigns, a larger turnout should come. The basic problem with this campaign has been that no one knew what to do or how to do it, and few had very much enthusiasm about it.

Isaac is starting a new voter registration drive, beginning Monday. He thinks he will be able to register twenty new voters a week. It is a long, slow process, but one day more Negroes than whites will be registered. One day, more Negroes than whites will vote. One day Negroes will be elected. One day Negroes will control Baker County. But that time is still a good ways off.

July 18

The days I write in the journal seem to be getting farther apart. Perhaps I'm growing a little weary, a little tired of the routine, a little less perceptive and enthusiastic.

The fact is that the summer is at a midpoint and things seem to be standing still. Head Start is not getting any easier. In fact, if anything, it is getting harder. The first four weeks of Head Start went well, but the second four are presenting a greater challenge, which as of yet we have not really begun to meet. The children no longer enjoy playing with the same old games and toys. They are getting more and more rowdy and need new challenges and special supervision. They are receiving neither. Most of the aides spend the major part of the day sitting, lounging, and talking. The teachers have not taken the initiative needed to change the daily routine more toward group games and activities. I enjoy working with the children, but they are really wearing me out. I have the midsummer slump and feel the need for a break from it all.

If Head Start is having its slump, the movement in Baker is going backward. Last evening only around twenty-five people were at the mass meeting, and those who were present did not show much concern about the election or anything else. Charlie pleaded and scolded, but it didn't do much good. The problem is that Head Start and the other gains that have been made—i.e., more decent treatment by whites—have been a real pacifier for the Negroes. No one seems to feel the urgent need to keep the movement going, especially if it means more risks and sacrifices.

I can sympathize with both the local people, who now are feeling gains from last summer's conflict, and with the SNCC people, who are very exasperated with the apathy. So much *could* be done, if only someone would do it.

The ASCS elections are coming up, with the deadline for nominating new candidates being August 25. A lot of work *must* be done if Negroes are to get on the boards; but no one seems to be very interested.

There is still a chance to file a lawsuit against Sheriff Warren Johnson. Only two people have signed the affidavit, for which three names are required. It is almost incredible how slowly things happen and how difficult it is to effect change. I really feel for those working full-time on voter registration and community organization. It is easy to see why so many become cynical or give up. Fortunately *we* have Head Start, with all its pains and rewards, to occupy most of our time. Yet the lack of action and response still gets to us, and it is very discouraging.

The third factor in the midsummer slump is the religious situation. The revival last week was in many ways the most disturbing thing I have seen in Baker County. Each service begins with a prayer meeting, including songs, scripture reading, and several prayers, all chanted with a sense of urgency, with the congregation participating with A-men's, shouts, moans, and songs. This part of the service is mystifying and in its own way quite beautiful. However, when the preacher starts to preach, the beauty is lost in what becomes to my thinking a horror show. Over the course of forty-five minutes to an hour and a half, he rants and raves nonsense slogans and religious phrases until the congregation is worked up into a frenzy, shouting "A-men" to every word he says. On two evenings several people began screaming and hollering and jumping about so wildly that they had to be fanned or carried out. It is a strange and perverted form of religion that capitalizes on the sense of inferiority of blackness.

When the people break down, one can sense the psychological destruction that has been caused by segregation. It is a very pitiful sight to see—the old people crying and wailing and pleading with God to save them.

Some things I like, such as the casualness, spontaneity, and responsiveness of the people. But the religious service stands as a symbol of the past more than anything else I have seen here—paternalism, slavery, and inferiority. For this reason I believe it must be changed, and it will be when the Negro begins to feel worth and dignity. Why people like the Holts, Williams, Broadways, Millers, etc. still accept and love the old forms of worship is due to cultural conditioning I suppose. It is the only form of religion they have ever known. Perhaps they can't—and shouldn't—change. But what about the next generation, Bobby Broadway, Jackie Holt, Nathaniel Holt, etc.? I don't believe any of them will stick with it. I can certainly see why no SNCC workers have. [*Charles Sherrod, Martin Luther King Jr., and the SCLC leadership were clear exceptions.*] I can also see how in the coming years there may be a place in the Negro church for people like me. Maybe there will be a place in the white church for Negroes. This is what I want to work for. [*Unfortunately, churches remain one of the most segregated institutions in our society today, perhaps because of the profound cultural and historical differences Joe was expressing above.*]

Friday, we had a full day taking the kids to the zoo in Albany.

Saturday, seven teenagers joined us in going to Koinonia Farm near Americus for a movement meeting. [*Koinonia Farm was another unusual integrated institution in Georgia that exists to this day. It was started in the 1930s by radicals—my Uncle Jack was involved in some way, as was President Jimmy Carter. Today they still live a simple communal life growing and selling pecans, and hosting visitors from around the world who want to learn about civil rights.*] We waited three hours at the SNCC house for the bus to come—same old SNCC house. But the meeting was OK. If only the SNCC "cats" would quit debating the ideals of Black Power and get down to some of the hard work, then something might really happen. There exists a type of "in group" attitude among the SNCC workers that seems to me to block communication with the local people. Sometimes I wonder if they really want anything positive to happen. It's all about how bad the whites are, when so few of the local Negroes have ever been touched by the movement. The movement is a long, slow, tedious, discouraging process that fails a thousand times more than it succeeds in giving the Negro a new possibility for becoming more fully human. But perhaps even one person who grows and "becomes free" justifies all the dull, tedious, weary hours of walking dusty roads, waiting for meetings, talking when you don't feel like it, and being very, very patient.

July 19

Yesterday evening we went into Albany for a meeting concerning the candidacy of C. B. King for U.S. Congress. A typically small group from Albany was at the mass meeting, and only three other counties were represented. This made the meeting less significant than what probably was expected. Twelve people came from Baker.

The meeting went very slowly, but it looks like C. B. will run. He needs a petition, signed by 5 percent of the registered voters, in order to be an independent candidate. Since a great deal of work will be required to get such a petition signed, it was decided that Wells should poll the other eighteen counties to see if they would support C. B. Not much else was done. Every time we go to Albany, we are reminded of how dead the movement is there and how lucky we are to be in Baker.

[*The following is a description of witnessing the trial of the man who murdered Grace Miller's husband the previous summer. C. B. King was Mrs. Miller's lawyer in a civil suit. As I recall, C. B. spent a great deal of time getting testimony that was unlikely to make a difference in the jury decision made in Baker but was likely to make a difference when he appealed the case to a higher court.*]

This afternoon after Head Start we went to the courthouse, where we heard C. B. King question various "crackers" concerning jury discrimination. Each man denied that he had ever discriminated against Negroes in relation to jury duty, even though no Negroes had ever been asked to serve—*and* even though each witness said he believed in white supremacy and segregation!

The courtroom was packed; and while we were there (all of us sat in the Negro section), we were as much a point of attention as the trial. [*The courtroom was still segregated—officially or unofficially. This was probably the most uncomfortable I felt all summer.*] The judge read a newspaper while several whites joked around with Sheriff Warren Johnson's son, Herbert.

This is the old way—the cold, bitter stares of whites, the stark segregation, the arrogant admission to being a segregationist, the open hatred of Negroes and of change. It is shocking to see, though you knew it was like this. My reaction was one of contempt and condescension. How could any people be so stupid! Yet, they are human beings. They are to be pitied more than the Negro. How could one have anything but *respect* for the Holts, Broadways, Williams, Millers, etc.? How could anyone not *pity* the Halls, the Johnsons . . . ?

July 20

Another day at trial. We sat in the Negro section from 1:30 until 5:30, watching C. B. King give the whites hell. The first part of the afternoon was spent questioning the jury. C. B. asked each white person if he felt whites were more inclined to tell the truth than blacks. Every man except one admitted that he did feel "whites were more truthful." (Two men went so far as to say no "Nigra" *ever* told the truth.) The white lawyer in turn would ask if they were prejudiced toward this "*particular* Nigra," whom no one knew. They all shook their head, no. C. B. King asked the judge to strike each man from the jury. The judge refused each time.

After two hours of this, the trial began. A young Negro was being tried for driving without a license. In the course of the trial, C. B. King got Herbert Johnson to admit that he never told the defendant that he was entitled to a lawyer, nor did he tell him he did not have to answer all his questions. C. B. pleaded for a mistrial and was refused. After about fifteen minutes of discussion, the jury returned and issued a verdict of guilty. Justice is nonexistent in Baker County. The judge announced there would be no more trials this session. There were sixteen civil rights cases left standing, including Mrs. Miller's suit against Cal Hall.

Cal Hall was the white man who shot Hosie Miller, a black man, in the back in cold blood a year ago last March in a dispute over a cow (a dispute in which he was in the wrong). He went scot-free, pleading self-defense, and in the back of his truck is carrying the same gun he shot Hosie with, the gun that he aimed last fall at the black kids who came to the white school. [*The Holt boys were a few of the black children who had integrated the white school the previous year, showing the bravery of the family.*] The murder of Mr. Miller set off the civil rights movement in Baker.

I learned this evening that Cal Hall is Mrs. Miller's cousin. Her father was the bastard son of "Old Man Hall," born to his Negro maid. Old Man Hall had four legitimate children, one of whom is Cal Hall.

The whole history of Baker County is incredible. Sheriff Warren Johnson, the large, scruffy old man who looks like Carlyle Marney [*a famous Protestant preacher of the time*], has killed so many Negroes it is difficult to count them all. He has shot at highway patrolmen who have entered the county. He is said to have run over two white women while driving 110 miles an hour, drunk. When his brother Ben, now a deputy, went into the army, Warren Johnson married Ben's wife, who was Warren's wife's sister. Warren never got a divorce from his first wife.

Warren Johnson shot a Negro in the bottom part of the county at a dance. The man was asleep in a car when the sheriff pointed his flashlight at him. Warren shot him in cold blood when the man protested being blinded. He killed the Sap boy (Bird Sap, a Negro who ran whisky for him). He also killed a Negro at Blue Springs when a white man was running around with the Negro's girlfriend. A dispute came up one day, and Warren shot the Negro. These are just some of the most recent murders.

Two years ago, Herbert Johnson, Warren's twenty-eight-year-old son and a deputy, killed a Negro whose girlfriend was a white man's mistress. And so it goes, on and on and on. I shake my head saying it couldn't happen, but I know that it is all true. The sins of the white man are so deep that there is no way they can possibly be righted.

July 25

The routine continues. Hot, sweltering weather prevails with afternoon temperatures usually over one hundred degrees. Long days at Head Start.

Thursday evening, we went to the revival at the Pleasant Grove AME Church in Newton. The preacher got no response during the first two-thirds of the sermon. All of a sudden, with no preparation and no apparent reason, he began shouting and chanting. After only a few minutes of this, the people began "getting happy" and going into convulsions. It is obviously nothing the preacher says but rather the tone of his voice that brings on the fits. I think of Pavlov and his dogs.

There is so much that is good mixed in with the bad. The Negroes are so free to express their deep feelings and emotions. They lay their hearts and emotions bare. The singing and the praying are for the most part very moving. So many strands are interwoven. Many of the songs are call-and-response chants. Others are the Negro spirituals. Still others are closer to current rock 'n' roll songs. It would be interesting to trace the various strands in the worship services.

Communion was held this Sunday at Pleasant Grove and last Sunday at St. Matthew's. Instead of being at the center of the service, as it is in Episcopal churches, communion came last after the sermon, offering, closing hymn, and even after the majority of the men had left!

The communion chants were quite moving, as was the freedom and spontaneity with which the communing occurred.

The minister at Pleasant Grove was not so offensive as Pickney. He read most of his sermon (which I could not follow) and received practically no response. About three-fourths of the way through it, he began chanting. The responses picked up but never approached the intensity of the St. Matthew's congregation's.

Ashley and Ann went to the white church, where they were generally ignored, except for the preacher's wife who greeted them very warmly until they identified themselves. Then her tone of voice changed and she quickly walked away.

Mrs. Foster introduced all of us, giving us a big buildup. She messed up information on everyone, but no one so much as Mimy, who attended "Adolf College in Macon, Georgia." Good old Mrs. Foster. At first I thought she was a real phony and a "Tom." But she isn't. She is just a very warm, vague, sort of out-of-it, naive woman, with a lot of love, compassion, and enthusiasm that is really sincere. She has been a good teacher to work under, though she lacks initiative and refuses to take leadership over the staff members in her room, most of whom have not really worked very hard. [*As I recall the summer, each classroom had a professional teacher—usually an elementary teacher from the school system. In addition the program had two out-of-town professional early childhood experts—as well as several nonprofessional aides such as ourselves.*]

Of the aides in our room, one is very good, and one is very bad and has really done absolutely nothing the entire summer. The other two are mediocre. Grace Kilpatrick has desire and motivation, but she does not have a lot of strength and consequently does not work as hard as Gwyn. She has improved, however, and is basically a good worker and a good person. I can't say as much for Mrs. Eddy, who at times plays with the children but most of the time sits around and does nothing. When asked to work, she will.

So in our room we have a staff of really just three, and sometimes four, workers, rather than six. That makes the situation more taxing than it should be, and at times the children really wear me out. They jump all over me, pull at my hair, hit me, and ask me to push them on the swings, jump them in the air, pull them in wagons, etc., all day long. The work, though often wearing, has been very rewarding. Many of the children have really grown in just these five weeks. I think of Denta, Mar Cole, Vivian, even Joe Louis Wallace. [*This little boy did not speak at all when the summer began. He slowly came out during the time we were there and, by the end of the summer, had begun speaking and interacting with other children. I believe, in retrospect, that he was emotionally disturbed.*] All of them have benefited from the program. They all play together much better, express themselves more freely, and are more creative. At first they were amazingly docile and timid. Though some have become "wild men," their ability to express this energy is very encouraging. They play harder, work better, and now even listen better than they did in the opening weeks. Our program has gradually changed from a full day of individual play to a more structured program of group activity, games, music, singing, and listening to stories. The children want to be together and play games when at first they did not, and they are beginning to enjoy listening to stories. All this is extremely important in preparing them for first grade. If Head Start were to stop today, it would have been a great success.

There are still challenges. Each child is an individual, and each child needs special attention. The variations in levels of development—already at age five—are startling. Some children like Wallace, Howard, or Denita are bored with working puzzles. Some like Joe Louis, Cal, or Mac can hardly even get one piece right. The children are all different and at different levels of intellectual and emotional growth.

The greatest problem is Pamela, who is extremely bright but who refuses to co-operate on anything. I think the heart of her problem is that she is spoiled and needs firm limits. Yet she has not really responded to much that we have done. She still knocks over paint, kicks down block houses that other children have made, refuses to play games, etc. I have tried to spend more time with her, and I think now I must be firmer. Others, such as Willie J., Judy, Cal, Brenda (who has only one eye), and Vivian, all have minor problems and need careful attention. I find it very hard to keep on top of it all. I feel as if I'm in a boxing ring and react as best as I can to the blows. Perhaps it would help if I kept a record on each of the twenty children, but I haven't. Nevertheless, the program has gone reasonably well in our class. Ann Runk has been the stabilizing influence and has kept the program moving on the right track. Her warmth and love for the children makes her a real inspiration to me.

The summer moves on and only three weeks remain. They will pass rapidly, and before we know it we'll be back in New York. We must not let these last few weeks drift away. Much still needs to be done. Yet things move so slowly and there seems so little that we can do. Attempts to get voter registration moving have never gotten off the ground. People just don't move fast. It is both frustrating and refreshing. There is something very healthy about taking one's own good time—a wisdom that says, what's the hurry? Life is not very long. Why kill yourself running helter-skelter? Relax, move at your own pace. Enjoy God's creation.

July 27

On the way to recovery after a three-day bout with a horrible cold and an infected foot. Mimy and I went into Albany today and saw a doctor—a white doctor since the Negro doctor does not see white folks!—who gave us a prescription for sulfur pills.

The past few days I have been rather miserable. I have stayed home while Mimy, who also has a mild cold and an infected leg, has gone to Head Start. I have tried to do a little reading, finally beginning Bonhoeffer's *Letters from Prison.* Inspiring. I realize how much in need of God's love I am. I realize *again* how this power is not within me. I just can't keep on giving. The children get me down, the routine wears me out, life has seemed to close in. Life is a continual reminder that I am unable to make it on my own, to make it living the full rich life that I want so much to live. I am unable to love anyone, not even Mimy—much less myself. I have really been horrible to Mimy, taking out my own frustrations and fears on her. [*I have long since forgotten!*] Sometimes I wonder how she tolerates me. And to think that she really loves me! Why is it so hard to return this love? At times I am just unable—as hard as I might try!—to respond. At the base of it all is my own egotism and self-centeredness. When I am more concerned about myself than Mimy, things just don't jive. Yet how does one break out of the pattern and really give oneself to another? Is this power within the power of the will? I don't know. I do know that I need God's help to really love, to forgive, and to be forgiven. I need God's strength to grow and become a man. God have mercy on me.

This week has also been the trial of Mr. Cal Hall, who is being sued by Mrs. Grace Miller for $340,792.10. Since I was sick, I missed the long tedious testimonies by Hall and the two other witnesses. Apparently as was to be expected, it has been another tragic farce. Hall claims he shot Mrs. Miller's husband in self-defense. The Negro witness swears

Hosie neither said nor did anything to provoke Hall, who shot him in cold blood over a disputed calf. Hosie had no gun, but was a big man weighing almost three hundred pounds. He also was a family man who had a prospering farm, five beautiful daughters, an unborn son, a brand new house, etc.

Attorney King made a brilliant, eloquent speech this afternoon, while the defending lawyer, L. Earl Jones, gave a typically intense diatribe. The whole situation is quite sickening: all-white jury, contradictory remarks by the defendant and the other white witnesses, and yet he will be acquitted in another travesty of the law. One becomes very aware of the hardness of heart of the white man. It is incredible how so many white people lie under oath.

The courtroom was about half full—almost all Negroes—who sat on the "white side"! A thunderstorm came up just as the concluding speeches began, making the scene quite dramatic.

Today I got my reward for all the effort I have put out for the children. As I came down the hall, one little child from another room grabbed my hand and said, "Hey, look, here he is." Before I could say anything all the kids in my class had come out of the room and were touching me and pulling on my hand. Their faces lit up as they smiled with puzzled expressions, "Hey, where you been? Where you been?" There they were: Joe Louis, Mac, Shelia, Faye, Cal, Wallace, Brenda, Denita, Willie J. Their warm smiles filled me with a realization that it all has not been in vain. The summer has been worthwhile. I have had my reward.

Thanks be to God.

July 28

Cal Hall is acquitted. Three hours of deliberation. Whites are happy. Negroes resigned. It was what everyone expected. Plans are being made for an appeal.

July 30

Only two more weeks remaining in Head Start. The summer is passing very fast. Last night was the final PTA meeting. It began with games and ended with a rather heated and confused debate concerning the CAP [*Community Action Program, the federally funded antipoverty program*] of Baker County. About half the Head Start staff and fewer than twenty parents were present.

At such times one becomes aware of how extremely difficult and complex change is. Most people—rich or poor, black or white—are generally apathetic about matters that don't directly concern them. And so it is in Baker County, where of the county's twenty-five hundred Negroes, fewer than seven hundred are registered voters, and fewer than one hundred are involved in the movement.

The debate last night was between the women and the men, the "radicals" and the "moderates," a division we have been vaguely aware of all summer. Mrs. Holt and Mrs. Miller are the key women, and Mr. Broadway and Mr. Williams, the key men.

The issue was over the community action panel, which is a group of whites and Negroes set up this spring to deal with community problems and apply for antipoverty program money. For some unknown reason, none other than L. Earl Jones was elected chairman. Mrs. Miller and Mrs. Holt have rightly protested this and the obvious fact that, with Jones as chairman and the other white representatives also being racists, nothing will be done by the committee. This has been shown to be the truth so far. Jones illegally made all the meetings closed meetings, and nothing has been done. Representatives from the federal government were here last week and darkened hopes for the child-care center, which Mrs. Holt and Ann Runk had planned. They also said whatever would be done must be done by the CAP and then submitted to a man in Moultrie [*a town in southwest Georgia*] who is head of a thirteen-county poverty area, of which Baker is a part. This means Baker can no longer go along with Albany. [*Presumably, Albany, being the largest city in southwest Georgia, and further along the integration path, would have been more favorable to the plans for a Baker child-care center.*]

So things are generally in a mess. No one knows what is going to happen. The only thing for certain is that, for now anyway, the CAP has to be given a chance. I see no way any real good can come from it, but it seems to be the only alternative. What a difficult struggle change is! If the antipoverty program is in such a jumbled mess everywhere else like it is here, how can it really effect change?

July 31

Many reflections. Many definite impressions are beginning to form.

Yesterday we attended another southwest Georgia staff meeting at Koinonia Farm outside of Americus. After the experience of sitting through the last staff meeting, only one local person, Pat James, decided to go with us. If the last meeting was frustrating and confusing, this one was even more so. From 4:30 to 6:30 and 7:30 to 10:45, there was a lot of arguing and debating over various confusing issues, the main one being the division of work in southwest Georgia.

It was extremely discouraging. For one thing, some of the SNCC workers seem to be way off base. They often handle the meetings in dictatorial fashion, not listening to other people and speaking in terms of a "great vision." Often it is very hard to follow or understand them. They just don't make sense. I can't exactly put my finger on what the problem is. I think they are very confused in their own minds as to what they want or where the movement should go. They show little concern for anyone—local people, SIM staff, or other SNCC staff. Yesterday was the low point to date. They have lost my respect.

What has happened? Have they changed? Or have the problems changed? Perhaps both. Now that demonstrations, pickets, sit-ins, etc. have passed, now that the long, hard work of registering voters, of welfare work, of federal programs, of organizing small committee meetings has begun, the old tactics of personal charisma won't work. What is needed is slow, steady hard work—most of which is not very sensational or rewarding. It is probably much less dangerous, but in many ways it is much more difficult. Criticizing whites alone won't work. There must be positive work—positive work within the Negro community, and positive work with the system—jobs, education, political power. These are the things people need. Protests have helped, but their value is decreasing. Emotional rallies have helped, but the people are weary of getting all riled up and seeing no positive results. This new stage of the movement requires new skills and insight. It demands the effective use of power within the system: ASCS elections, political elections, jobs—a big thing here is the antipoverty program. Some of the SNCC folks scorn this—they scorn Head Start—but they offer few positive alternatives. In many ways maybe Head Start is phony and only token action, but it *is* action and it has possibilities of reaching lots of people. And the Head Start program we are in seems to be working.

After all, what is the civil rights movement all about? It is a movement of human beings, who happen to be black instead of white, demanding equal opportunity to participate in the American system. Whenever this becomes perverted so that the movement becomes everything and the actual people become lost behind the idea, then a demonic influence takes over. This seems to be true in every revolution—the French Revolution, the Russian Revolution, etc. It is true here in southwest Georgia. The people—their needs and problems—must always be first, not the movement. What is not good for them, what does not put the people first, is perverse—regardless of the name it is called.

SNCC has a "vision," but that's all it is. They are wrapped up in the vision of the movement and consequently are out of touch with the needs of the people. Whatever the vision is, it often seems to be quite unrelated to the reality of helping human beings grow.

Here in Baker County there are many problems, the main one being the difficulty of living with the whites in a community of justice, equal opportunity, and peace. The Negroes—even the ones in the movement—are not primarily "movement people." They are primarily human beings who want to improve their community. The movement is one way they can see something begin to happen. The antipoverty program is now another way. The civil rights legislation and political power are more distant, but important. For the most part, however, these are just a small portion of their interests. The basic question they are concerned with is *How do I as a human being get along in life? How do I raise a good family, make a good living, live a good life?* Church, work, education are all as important as being in the movement. All play a part in living a good life.

If anything, I am becoming more tolerant of American so-called middle-class life. People aren't so different, regardless of where they live or work, or their color. We are all in search of the "good life," which takes a different form for each person. Few find it. But how can I really criticize all whites, or all bourgeois? Negroes are human beings. SNCC workers are human beings. And as humans, we are all in the same boat—and really no one is better than anyone else. Perhaps this is what original sin is all about. That humans are all fundamentally the same is just as obvious here as anywhere else. It is certainly obvious in the southwest Georgia staff meetings. There are no roads to salvation in anything we do. There is surely no salvation in the civil rights movement!! If there is any salvation, it is in God. It is a gift. There is nothing we can do to earn it. There is no one free from sin (self-centeredness, confusion, alienation). If nothing else, I have surely learned *this.*

I have also learned that I am not a revolutionary, or a "movement man," or a community organizer. If I pretend to be one, I am a real phony. I am a human being who sees certain evils existing and who wants to do something to help. But I have no desire to commit myself totally to the civil rights movement or any other movement. Nor do I have the stamina, ability, or willingness to be a full-time organizer or to commit myself to this work. Perhaps it is too much for me. Perhaps I am becoming aware of where my talents and abilities lie—or rather don't lie.

Where do my commitments lie? What positive has come out of this experience?

I enjoy working with these people here in Baker County. They are good people—very much themselves—honest, many quite strong. I like them very much and have come to feel a part of the community. We have not *done* a great deal. We have helped in Head Start and have done a pretty good job there. It has been wearing but fun and rewarding. We have done none of the community organizing that Ed, Joe, and Jim have done. We have exerted no leadership, given no talks in mass meetings, or—with the exception of Ashley—in church. In some ways I wish I could say I had done something; but I feel this is probably more ego needs than anything else. The important thing is not that we have *done* anything but rather that we have been here with the people and have shared their life and grown with them. There are no feathers to put in our hat for it (like "we've done this and this and this"), but there is a feeling in our hearts for many of the people here. We have come to love them, and we have felt their love for us. No, it has not been overwhelming or sensational; but there has developed a mutual respect, understanding, and affection.

After all, what is community organizing all about? It is living in a community and sharing the life of the people, helping them get the things they want and need and giving them resources and guidance when needed. The difficult thing is how much leadership should be exerted, how much the organizer should dictate, how much he should just suggest, how much he should do himself.

We have tried to suggest, but at no time have we dictated or done things by ourselves. Perhaps this has been our weakness. I think we could have assumed more leadership at times—especially on organizing voter registration.

But we are white. We are quite unfamiliar with such areas as politics, welfare, antipoverty programs, etc. And, most of all, we are here only for the summer. How can we, with any integrity, claim that we know *any* answers to any of the problems? We came to learn what the problems are, to help where we were needed, and to give of ourselves. We were needed in Head Start. Obviously, we perhaps could have done much more in other areas, but under the circumstances, I can say we have done the best we could.

There are no easy answers. There is no fast progress anywhere. People are people everywhere. Human nature is what it is. I am still attracted to the ministry—perhaps more so after the summer. I feel it will give me the freedom to act responsibly, and with integrity, while preserving my sanity. I want to serve God, though that's about all I can say about religion at this time. I want to love Mimy and to love other people, too. I want to share God's love.

I don't enjoy going to church. Perhaps I will grow in that area [*as he did, becoming an active church member in middle age*]. God give me the strength to stick with it.

August 3

The last entry I recorded was that we had really come to love the people, and they us. What I suppose I really meant was we had come to love the Holts. This word may be inaccurate here. After all, what is love?

However, concerning our relationships with the rest of the people, if anything, there has been a lack of close relationships. We are close to Ann and Ashley, but we aren't close as a staff. We never see Mickey or Larry [*the other white seminary "married" couple working there*]. More important, no one has formed close relationships with any of the local people in Head Start. Mrs. Josie Miller is very friendly; the others are cordial. But there have been few real friendships formed. If anything there may be quite a bit of hostility. I have had few conversations with any of the aides in my room. In fact, we rarely exchange words. Mimy today felt that she was being ignored by the aides in her room because she "told on them to Ann." If this is true, it is very sad. So near the end of the program and the question is raised, what good have we done? Perhaps we've done more harm than good.

[*It is interesting that Joe portrays our social relationships this way, because— looking back more than forty years—I have a very happy memory of the summer socially. It was a rare feeling to be living with a close family who loved us, and we them. That warmth of feeling has stayed with me my whole life, and has rarely been experienced again. While we were not close to other people, I felt very accepted by the Broadways and Millers. In addition we became extremely close to Ashley and have kept up that relationship to this time (although we rarely see him, as is also the case with Ed Feaver and Joe Pfister). Unfortunately, we have completely lost touch with everyone else over the years.*]

First of all, we have done a good job with the kids. We have worked hard and related to them quite satisfactorily. But in so doing, we have perhaps put ourselves in competition with the local people. I have not put out much effort to get to know any of them. Here we have missed a real opportunity and have made a serious mistake. Our being in Head Start could have benefited the staff as well as the children. As it is, we have not built up a trust or a good relationship. The main reason has been that we (I) just have not cared. There is no excuse for it. It is our own pride standing in the way. It is our own prejudice. I think all of us have looked down on the other aides. All of us feel that we are better. All of us have been trying to prove we are better. Certainly this holds true for me.

[*I also have a somewhat different take on this from Joe (again looking back over a long period of time and writing from recollection). I believe my own point of view was that my job was to serve the children and help them grow and learn over the summer. I viewed that as more important than relating to or teaching the aides. I think either job would have been worthwhile, but it was not possible to do both since they were somewhat in conflict. The aides were not trained child-care workers; and I don't know their educational level, but it wasn't high. So they understandably didn't know how to do the job and could not learn so quickly with just a small amount of training. They were not very energetic with the children, because they hadn't grown up treating children in the way that Head Start was trying to do (using modern child-care development principles). So we were better able to learn from Ann Runk and—I think—really help the kids. Many of them changed dramatically over the summer.*]

We have some very good people in our room. Gwyn is excellent. Grace has really improved. Even Carrie has come along and really helped today. But only now am I aware of my failure in not relating to them. Only a week left. Perhaps it is not much time, but I will sure try to go out of my way. This lack of sensitivity is one of my basic weaknesses anyway. This is just one of its many manifestations.

Various impressions: Sitting on the porch on a rainy evening. Mr. Holt rambles on talking about tracking hogs. Absolutely incredible. His mind recalls the most minute details, and he tells stories with enthusiasm and with mannerisms that are impossible to paraphrase or describe.

We were to go to Damascus Church to a revival, but finally were told not to go. Revivals and church are the only social life Negroes have during the summer. No wonder the church is important. It is the only outlet. [*This implies we were unwelcome at the social event, but I do not recall any feelings of exclusion from social events of this type because of our race that summer.*]

August 7

Late Sunday evening. The past few days have been very wearing and frustrating. Mimy, Ashley, and I stayed here instead of going to Cordele and Dawson for various meetings. There were many reasons, the main two being the extreme inconvenience of traveling 130 miles round-trip and the dislike of the meetings in general. We drove Mrs. Holt to Albany in her new car and got more medicine for Mimy's infection.

Today, however, things were different. We started the day off by going to the white church. No incidents, though we were generally avoided. Many thoughts here, but no time to record them now. [*So this is lost to history, since I have only the vaguest of recollections of a rather boring church service, and extreme discomfort at being in a place where we were not wanted.*]

Then we learned of a SIM meeting to be held at Mrs. Josie's. Though it started two hours late, the meeting was decent. At last some of the hostilities came out. Ashley spoke the most, but I got a lot off my chest, too. Still, much went "unsaid." Some of our coworkers' attitudes disturb me. They talk of how revolutionaries must have total commitment. While I respect them, I dislike their attitude of superiority and their scorn of others who don't have that total commitment. I realize *I am no revolutionary!*

One hundred people attended the mass meeting. Three hundred and thirty-one dollars was collected for Mrs. Miller. Still things went very slowly and dragged on. ASCS, finances, etc.

Charlie was friendly. He went out of his way to strike up a conversation—his way of saying, "It's OK." For the first time, I felt a feeling of "it's OK"—it's been a good summer.

Still, I wonder what will become of the Southwest Georgia Project.

August 8

Because the Head Start program is out of funds, Friday was the last day the buses ran, and last Wednesday was the last day anyone got paid. Today thirteen out of twenty children in our class made it to school via parental transportation, and in all fifty-three out of 120 children came to school. This shows that the program really has meant something to the children and their parents. It is very encouraging. It is also encouraging that practically all the staff is working for one and a half weeks without pay.

This afternoon—for the first time this summer—I got a group of teenagers to work on voter registration. The big problem has been that we have had no transportation. Today Jitty had Mr. Broadway's car, and we used it. Trisha James was really the spark plug of the group. She knew people who had not registered. We drove to their houses and in all got three people to register. We drove them to the registrar's office, where the whole procedure was short and simple. One of the men had tried to register in 1963, when he was asked to recite all the American presidents *in order.*

Here it is, August 8, and we have registered the first people. If only we had started earlier, but we tried. No car, no co-operation, and perhaps not enough initiative from us. And it takes *time*. It takes time until you are trusted. It takes time until you have any idea what should be done. It takes time until you feel people are ready, and then you are never sure. It is a very difficult tightrope that you must walk, between going too fast or being too pushy, and not doing a damn thing.

The civil rights movement seems to grow more complex as the days roll on. First of all, there are the local people the civil rights workers are trying to help. The local people, however, can be divided into groups ranging from "Toms" to "Snickites." Just like any community anywhere, all kinds of unique human beings are present, so that if one is honest one cannot easily say *the* Negro in Baker wants this or this or this. As the movement has progressed here, division and hostilities have become more obvious. The east of the county versus the west; the men versus the women; the radicals versus the moderates. The Williamses versus Mrs. Holt. Mrs. Holt's and Mrs. Josie's competition for leadership. The supporters of Isaac versus Sherrod's supporters. And so it goes in the movement. And the movement is but a small minority of the people in Baker County. Pineland, Bene Acres, Pine Bloom, etc., are untouched. [*These are various plantations; I am not sure of the spelling and I only remember Pineland.*] Bethany and Hoggins Mill are still isolated from the central section, etc. Geographic boundaries tend to separate.

There are many people in the county whom the movement has never touched. Many of the old farmers, for instance, who are still living as if they were in slavery. I think of the plantation workers, Bo Holt, Big Mama Holt, many of the people in church. And yet this group I know least, so I really don't know how they feel.

So much for the local movements. Next come the SNCC workers who mosey in and out with Isaac, talking of Black Power and speaking to no one. When Isaac works, he is very good, but he is sporadic. He wastes much time. He has difficulty making decisions. But he is patient, and he is a pragmatist. As for the others, I have never seen them do a damn thing. I think Isaac's approach is very good, but it is slow; and he, too, is very different from the local people.

And there are many more factions: SCLC, C. B. King, the lawyers, the Georgia Council, the antipoverty programs and the CAPs, and last of all SIM, which as far as I'm concerned means only volunteers who came down with Charlie—white, naive, and inexperienced.

How all these work together is something I do not really understand. That they work together at all is a miracle. If God is in the civil rights movement, it is in the fact that there is any movement at all.

The question of commitment that Ed brought up is still unsettling; I do not have the commitment to the movement that Ed has. I don't think I want it.

I am committed to many things to varying degrees. If there is anything I am most committed to, it is the task of living. As far as being committed to the civil rights movement, insofar as I see it as a viable means of helping alleviate human suffering, or helping change an unjust system for the better, I'll back it and work for it. When it becomes destructive and becomes an end in itself, I'll fight it. It is not God!

August 9

The summer in southwest Georgia is drawing to a close. Wednesday was the last day for the children. Yesterday we cleaned up and had a party for the Holts and Broadways. Today we are going to our last staff meeting in Moultrie. I suddenly feel very sad that we are going home soon. I am just beginning to realize the value of the experience. I am just beginning to realize how great the summer has been, how much I have learned, how much we have come to love Baker County and the people.

It has not been easy. The most difficult thing has been maintaining my relationship with Mimy under the living conditions of no privacy, not much recreation, very little time to ourselves. There have been quite a few tense moments, but we have managed to work through most of the conflicts and grow. Are we growing toward or away from each other? [*After forty-plus years of marriage, I think I can say that the answer to Joe's question is now evident! However, in those days people did not "live together" before marriage, so in so many ways we were just getting to know each other intimately.*] At times it has seemed we were growing away from each other, but I feel that now we are closer and more in love than at the beginning of the summer. It is different—less romantic infatuation and more respect. It is difficult to say a great deal more. We now realize that married life *is* different from single life. You need more privacy, security, and a place of your own. These are not just "middle-class" values. They are human needs. People are people everywhere. No wonder when people get married they settle down. You can't have a home and a marriage without a certain amount of stability. If anything, I have become more tolerant of my fellow noncommitted, noninvolved Americans.

Also accounting for many of the conflicts is the fact that we have both felt frustration at not being on top of the situation. The work at Head Start has often been frustrating. Attempts at voter registration and community organization have gotten nowhere. We have generally been anxious in not knowing what our place or role was. Were the whites plotting against us? Did the Negroes accept us? Were we doing what Sherrod and the SIM group wanted? Were we doing *anything* right? When one is uncertain of one's role in society, the frustrations are taken out on the person one loves most.

There have been ups and down: days when everything went right, days when nothing went right, days when we were very much in love, days when we were separated and estranged. It has been a summer just like life is anywhere, except that—because of the situation—many of the conflicts have been aggravated; and many of the feelings of love and hate have been intensified.

The work in Head Start has been very rewarding. I never thought working with five- and six-year-olds could be so stimulating and so challenging. These children have grown so much in these ten weeks. It is amazing. They have learned to express themselves in many ways—in painting, drawing, building, playing out of doors, speaking, etc. Each child has his or her own special talents. Each child is a unique human being with a definite and apparent potential. And each child has come in some way, often small, to realize this potential. Howard paints and dances beautifully; Wallace is a leader; Omar has a warmth and a glow (he was the shyest at first); even Joe Louis has learned to play with others. All the children have learned each others' names. They have learned to eat with utensils, to participate in group games, to sing songs, to play with one another, and to share. The progress they have made and the response they have shown have made the summer worthwhile many times over.

The party at the Broadways' last evening was a grand success. I cooked the steaks, which turned out to be delicious. Ann's presents were very, very clever. Mrs. Holt was so thrilled. Mrs. Josie came and ate with us. Everyone had a wonderful time. It was another reward for a summer of struggle and patience. We will never forget the Holts, or the Broadways, or Mrs. Josie.

Mr. Holt and I drove downtown today and did some errands. I cashed a check at the bank. No trouble. We went to the drugstore together, and as usual people were nice enough. Then we went to the courthouse and asked the county clerk (in a closed room where we met six whites sitting around shooting the bull) for a map. The white men were cordial, though they had no maps.

Ashley has had a couple of run-ins. Last Saturday he was cursed by an "old codger." But Mimy and I have had no unpleasant encounters. I think of how afraid we were at first of even showing our face in Newton. Now Mr. Holt and I can go into the courthouse together and nothing happens. Now I think nothing of walking in Newton alone or in an integrated group. Last Monday we took the kids to the post office, walked around the courthouse together, and were even given a demonstration of the fire engine by a smiling, white chief of police. Of course, hatred and bitterness still remain. Of course there are whites who would harass or even kill us if given the chance. White people still call Mr. Holt "Jack," which really makes me sick. [*At that time in the rural South, and still today in the African American community, it was a sign of disrespect to call someone of an older generation by their first name. We always called the adults we met by their last name, and they called us by our first, since we were just "kids." However, at that time very distinguished black people were called by their first names by whites, no matter what their ages. I fear that this still happens today.*] But most of the white people in Newton and probably in Baker, I feel, want peace and order and perhaps even want to do the right thing—though their thinking of what is right is little more than "be nice to niggers," so they won't march. It is the few such as Warren Johnson, Cal Hall, and Earl Jones who are dangerous, because the moderate whites have given them an "OK signal." The moderate whites are still to blame, for Johnson and clan become their henchmen, doing the dirty work for them. The fact remains, however, that for the most part, the summer has gone smoothly for us in our "relationship" with the whites. Perhaps things are getting better—though I realize that if there were no witnesses, or a confrontation, anything could happen. You still have to be careful!

August 15

In a few minutes we'll be leaving. I am sitting on the porch with Mr. Holt and Mr. Broadway, who are talking about plowing peanuts. It is quiet and peaceful. So quiet and peaceful that I shudder to think of New York. Mimy and I are very sad to be leaving.

The past few days have been encouraging, especially concerning the movement in southwest Georgia and the Southwest Georgia Project. The meeting Friday afternoon, though starting four hours late, went much better than the other staff meetings. Charlie was friendly. He let Isaac lead the meeting. He listened to others. He wasn't pushy. John Baptiste kept quiet and listened to others. People spoke up. Definite plans were made for going into new counties. For the first time, I could sense a feeling of togetherness, of purpose, of direction. The movement is finally beginning to take hold in southwest Georgia.

Saturday we canvassed all day in Albany, getting signatures for C. B. King and lining up voter registration. Between us, Mimy and I got twenty-five people to agree to be picked up on Wednesday; and more than fifty people signed King's petition [*to get his name on the ballot for the congressional election*]. That evening we bowled a final game with Ed, Ashley, Charlie, and Chris.

Sunday Ashley preached a terrific sermon at White Corner CME church on Pineland on "strength" (i.e., voter registration). We had already been to the best Sunday school session of the summer, where Bobby Broadway and Mrs. Hammond argued over civil rights versus the Negroes' duty to love white men. The service at White Corner was the best of the summer. Though fewer than fifty people were present, the Holy Spirit had stayed around after the sermon by Rev. "Welsh" [*another deformation that summer of Ashley's last name, Wiltshire*]. Sherrod made a plea for the next mass meeting to be held there. Several people, especially a middle-aged woman, argued emotionally in favor of Charlie's proposal. No one spoke against it. The visitors (we) left while the deacons debated. We later heard that they refused the request. There is still lots of talk, but many people are too afraid to stick their necks out. [*On Pineland, and the other plantations, most people were sharecroppers or laborers and didn't own their own house or property—in contrast to the independent black farmers who were involved in the movement. The sharecroppers could have been evicted from their homes and lost their jobs at any time.*] Nevertheless, a spirit was present during the service that made me very happy for the future of the movement in Baker County and very sad to be leaving.

The mass meeting that evening was well attended (seventy-five people or so) and typically slow. The Grace Miller fund [*for her lawsuit against her husband's murderer*] was added up. She now has $1,150.00. Now we are on a bus going to Atlanta. We will miss Baker County, the Holts, and the other folks a great deal. It has been a tremendous summer. Our opinion of the Southwest Georgia Project has run the gamut, from optimism, to despair, to optimism and hope. We now see possibilities beginning to emerge, and hope forming. Charlie has regained control. Long-range plans are being developed. A long, hard path lies ahead. But now I think the movement might just make it.

PART III

Aftermath, 1966–1968

Chapter Ten:
Back to New York

W e emerged from our summer in southwest Georgia and returned
to school forever changed. We did not have a gradual transition
but were immediately plunged back into the southern culture in which
we had grown up. On our way back to New York, we stopped in
Conway, South Carolina, to attend Embry's brother's wedding. D. G.
Martin was a Yale law student at the time and engaged to Harriet Wall,
whose father was a large landowner and businessman in South Carolina.
We had mixed feelings about going to the wedding. On the one hand,
Embry loved her brother, who shared our values and was progressive
about political and social issues, as was Harriet. On the other hand, this
was to be a southern society wedding. And South Carolina was not far
ahead of southwest Georgia when it came to race, as I had witnessed in
the attitudes of some of my fraternity brothers who were from there.
It might be awkward.

The wedding was fun—an elegant service in the Presbyterian
church, a lavish reception under a huge tent, delicious southern food,
champagne flowing, a lively band, dancing, and a cast of several hundred
well-wishers. Still, for us there was a disconnect. All the waiters were
black. As was the custom, the African Americans in attendance—mostly
those who worked for the Wall family—sat in the balcony away from
the white guests. All the other attendees were white like us. I recalled
that the wedding of Joe Howell and Embry Martin, which had occurred
just six months earlier, followed the same rules. While this made us
uncomfortable at the time, we did not do a thing to change it.

Yet our thinking was different now. We were just coming off the front lines of the civil rights movement. We had been on the black side of the fence fighting against segregation, and here we found ourselves back on the white side of the fence. Whose side were we on?

I found myself enjoying the festivities, but I struggled to understand what that meant. We could walk back through the gate into the world of white privilege that we had grown up in, and no one would really notice. That gate was closed to the black farmers like the Holts and Broadways and the SNCC organizers. Did this mean we were phonies to go down there and pretend we were making a difference? Did it mean that we should have stayed at home and not gotten involved in the first place? Did it mean that it was wrong to go back to our white world, and should we have boycotted the wedding out of principle?

I finally realized that as hard as I might try to pretend otherwise, I had grown up on the white side of the fence. I could not deny my past or who I was. I told myself that what it meant was that we had to accept who we were. We had to work harder to make America a place where the door could open in both directions.

★★★

We arrived in New York via train on a hot, sticky September day in 1966. This was the beginning of a new chapter in our lives, which turned out to be one of the best years in my life and certainly one of the most fun. The spring before we left for southwest Georgia, I had decided to take a year off from Union. The study of theology was beginning to get to me; and in a moment of inspired insight, I realized that I had no idea what any of my professors were talking about. They could very well have been lecturing in Chinese. I needed a break. The decision to take a break came at an awkward time, because the day before I had made a speech to the entire Union Seminary student body as to why I should be elected their vice president. The next day I announced that I would not be returning to the seminary. A little embarrassing, you might say. Some people said they thought I was unstable. Most, I believe, secretly envied me.

The decision was also liberating but not as liberating as the frank discussion I had with the Episcopal bishop of the Diocese of Tennessee. I had been under the care of my bishop for over a year and was a "postulant" —a candidate for ordination into the Episcopal priesthood, assuming I performed satisfactorily in seminary, passed canonical exams, and generally behaved myself.

The bishop was short, fit, and thin. He had white hair, a perpetual twinkle in his eye, and was feisty. He would come to New York to visit his various seminarians each year and take us all out to a fancy New York restaurant. All the other seminarians were at General Seminary in Lower Manhattan. I was the only postulant from Tennessee ever to attend Union. The bishop would hold forth on various topics, mostly theological, and down the first of several martinis, which often served as his meal. Usually after dinner we would go out to a club for entertainment. To the dismay of the other seminarians, the bishop often insisted that I sit at his right side.

When I got up my courage and told the bishop during our annual counseling session that I would be taking a year off from seminary, he turned bright red, as he often did, pounded his fist on the table, and shouted, "Dammit, Howell, why can't you play by the rules?"

"OK," he continued. "Do it your way, but when your next adventure is over, you are going to do it *my* way; and for every year you have spent in this infidel, heretical, Protestant seminary, you are going to spend a year in rehab at Nashoda House." Nashoda House, situated in rural Wisconsin, was an Anglo-Catholic Episcopal seminary where liturgical discipline was paramount. He knew there was no way I would ever agree to this. He had given me a respectable way out. I felt like a huge weight had been lifted from my shoulders. Despite his stern language, he could not hide a slight smile. We both knew what was going on.

The program that I participated in that year was called Metropolitan Urban Service Training (MUST), and it was designed for seminary students like me who were burned out. Eight students—mostly from Union—participated in our group, which was directed by a fine Episcopal priest, Dick Gary. We were expected to get secular jobs and meet weekly for discussion and reflection. I remember most the supportive atmosphere, the earnest participants, and the kindness and insight of Father Gary.

I held an eclectic mix of temporary jobs—editor of a millionaire's memoir, clerk, sales manager in Macy's toy department during the Christmas rush, and, best of all, counselor and driver for an after-school play group called Shelly's All Stars. Embry spent that year studying at Barnard and Columbia; and we tried to go to as many museums and as many free concerts and events as we could, which were a lot, since people were always giving away tickets for use by Union students. We really got to know New York City—or at least Manhattan. Slowly, our civil rights journey was becoming part of our past. While we followed, from a distance, what was happening in southwest Georgia and kept up with events nationally in the civil rights movement, we were no longer as engaged as we had been.

What was going on nationally were big changes; and by the fall of 1966, the issues and events that had dominated the movement for the first half of the decade had been replaced by an entirely new set of issues. The two major victories—the Civil Rights Act of 1964 and the Voting Rights Act of 1965—had addressed many of the most egregious wrongs. Blacks could now usually eat where they wanted to, go where they wanted to, and vote when they wanted to. And they were being elected to public office. School desegregation was still slow, but little by little school districts were integrating, often through busing. The problem was that the day-to-day life of many African Americans had not changed much. Many were still poor, had low-paying jobs and poor education, lived in substandard housing, and attended segregated schools. Some of the neighborhoods—especially the large ghettos in big cities—were rife with crime, full of dilapidated buildings, and segregated. Police brutality was pervasive. Many blacks still endured racial insults and were discriminated against in jobs and housing. Expectations were way up, but the facts on the ground were still grim. Antipoverty programs were slowly finding their way to local communities, but the process was cumbersome, often fought by the local officials, and grossly underfunded for the work that needed to be done. In short, the situation was ripe for exploitation and for disaster.

Other factors also were changing the landscape, chief among them the Vietnam War. The number of U.S. soldiers there had reached two hundred thousand by 1965, and young men were subject to the draft. In 1966, as troop levels continued to build and casualties increased, CORE issued a report claiming that the U.S. military draft placed "a heavy discriminatory burden on minority groups and the poor" and called for a withdrawal of all U.S. troops from Vietnam. The War on Poverty was competing with the Vietnam War for resources and losing. The antiwar movement on college campuses was beginning to coalesce about that time, redirecting student interest from the Deep South to Vietnam.

The leadership of the civil rights movement was also changing. Stokely Carmichael had replaced John Lewis as head of SNCC, and most of the earlier SNCC leaders had departed by the end of 1966. Carmichael himself stepped down from SNCC a year later and was replaced by H. Rap Brown. When Carmichael left SNCC for the Black Panther Party, Brown renamed the organization the "Student *National* Coordinating Committee." Nonviolence was no longer part of the SNCC mantra. Brown himself left SNCC the next year to become the minister of defense for the Black Panthers.

The Black Panther Party was started in Oakland in the fall of 1966 by Bobby Seale and Huey Newton. Centered on a loose black nationalist agenda, during the late 1960s it had about five thousand members. Though black nationalist and controversial because of its in-your-face posturing and its threats of violence, the party was relatively diverse. Socialism was also one of its causes and was emphasized to varying degrees depending on the times and who was in charge, with a strong social outreach program focusing on economic justice issues and helping the poor. FBI Director J. Edgar Hoover said the party posed "a great threat to the internal security of the country."

SCLC continued to promote nonviolence and focus on implementing the Civil Rights Act of 1964 and the Voting Rights Act of 1965. In the summer of 1966, one of its affiliates in Grenada, Mississippi, the Grenada County Freedom Movement, organized mass demonstrations, registered more than one thousand black voters, and enrolled black children at previously all-white schools, actions answered with arrests and beatings.

SCLC also turned its attention to the North, where de facto segregation was the major problem rather than Jim Crow laws. Its first target was Chicago, where it joined forces with the Coordinating Council of Community Organizations to protest discriminatory housing and hiring practices and poor city services. The initiative, called the Chicago Freedom Movement, set out with the ambitious agenda of ridding the city of slums, enlisting the support of whites as well as blacks. Jesse Jackson was appointed head of SCLC's Chicago initiative, Operation Breadbasket, which sought to overcome poverty in the black community. Marches were conducted in white as well as black neighborhoods, and more than sixty thousand people attended a rally at Soldiers Field, where Martin Luther King Jr. addressed the crowd.

Eventually the Chicago Freedom Movement won concessions from the city to open up housing opportunities for blacks throughout metropolitan Chicago. However, the northern initiative proved to be much more difficult than the southern campaigns, with more elusive goals. Enlisting mass support was more challenging. The problems were rooted in both race and economics. While the federal government was trying to address the latter with the War on Poverty programs, the resources allocated were far below what was required to effect real change. The slums of Chicago remained intact.

The NAACP focused primarily on legal issues and was quiet during this period. The National Urban League turned its attention to grassroots education initiatives. CORE started supporting international black nationalist causes, and its role as a national civil rights player gradually diminished. So by early 1967, the broad coalition of civil rights groups that had championed civil rights and focused the national eye on the evils of segregation had fallen apart. It was a new era.

What was getting the national attention was a different kind of civil rights activity. It had several names—civil disturbances, civil disorders, or, as called by most white people, "race riots." The difference between a civil disturbance or riot and the mass demonstrations that were part of so much of the civil rights movement was that civil disturbances were disorganized, leaderless, often spontaneous, and involved violence, usually by both participants and the police. Often the participants did not have specific goals in mind.

There had been a number of riots in America before the late 1960s: anti–Catholic riots, anti–German riots, antidraft riots, and a host of others. But in the 1960s the disturbances were mainly centered on race issues, and most took place in the large ghettos of the North, Midwest, and West Coast. Though there had been outbreaks of violence in cities as diverse as Cambridge, Maryland, in 1963 and Harlem, Rochester, and Philadelphia in 1964, these were relatively small and confined to neighborhoods. They did not get the nation's attention until 1965, when violence engulfed Watts, a section of Los Angeles with some thirty-five thousand residents, mostly black.

In 1964, the passage of the Civil Rights Act gave the black community reason for hope. A year later, in Watts there was little evidence that anything had changed or was going to change. The problems in Watts were exacerbated by a white backlash in California, where the passage of Proposition 14 had just blocked several fair housing provisions of the Rumsford Fair Housing Act, a state law against discrimination in housing. A routine traffic stop on August 11, 1965, ignited rock-throwing at police, the torching of buildings, the overturning of cars, looting, and gunfire. When it was over five days later, thirty-four people were dead, more than one thousand wounded, four thousand arrested; and hundreds of buildings had been destroyed. The governor of California, Pat Brown, established a special commission to study the riot and why it happened. Months later the panel reported that the riot had not been instigated by anyone, and that the causes were essentially poverty and racism. It should have been a wakeup call.

Two years passed after Watts. Embry and I finished the MUST year away from Union and were traveling in Europe, using the small inheritance I had received when my grandmother died a year earlier. I remember in early August thumbing through magazines at a newsstand in Paris that carried English-language periodicals. The cover of *Time* silhouetted a black figure carrying a television set with a burning building in the background. The caption was, "The Fire This Time." The reference was to a famous essay by novelist James Baldwin, "The Fire Next Time," in which Baldwin predicted catastrophe if America did not face up to its problems of race and poverty. I was stunned. What was going on? I immediately purchased the magazine, and Embry and I poured over the story. It was about the two major riots that had occurred the previous month—the first in Newark and the second in Detroit.

Newark erupted on July 12, 1967, under circumstances eerily like Watts: white police officers arrested a black cabdriver and dragged him into the precinct station, which was across the street from a large public housing project. Residents who witnessed the event, and whose experience, as in Watts, had led them to mistrust police, thought the cabdriver had been killed (in fact he had been injured and taken to the hospital). Six days later twenty-six people were dead, more than seven hundred wounded, and fifteen hundred arrested. Property damage was estimated to exceed $10 million.

The Detroit violence occurred less than two weeks later and was sparked by a police raid of a popular, unlicensed after-hours bar on Saturday, July 27. Before it was over five days later, forty-three people were dead, over four hundred injured, seventy-two hundred arrested, and more than two thousand buildings had burned to the ground. It remains the single most destructive urban disorder in American history. The *Time* story Embry and I read also mentioned smaller events occurring in June and July in Tampa Bay, Houston, Buffalo, and a host of other cities. From my vantage point in Europe, it seemed that the whole country was on fire.

The situation had radically changed in just over a year. The focus had shifted from the South to the rest of the country and from small towns and rural counties to urban ghettos. Civil rights leaders seemed to be powerless in these disturbances, which were leaderless and seemed to have a mind and an energy all their own. Whites and blacks also viewed them very differently, with whites blaming the participants and blacks blaming the white power structure for allowing deplorable living conditions to exist.

President Johnson responded by setting up a national blue-ribbon commission on July 28, during the Detroit uprising. Named for its chairman, the governor of Illinois, the panel included business, civil rights, and government leaders. Seven months later, at the end of February 1968, the Kerner Commission issued the "Report of the National Advisory Commission on Civil Disorders," which came to be known simply as "The Kerner Report." The report's most famous passage stated bluntly, "Our nation is moving toward two societies, one black, one white—separate and unequal." It cited racism as a major cause of the disorder and called for massive federal action to create better jobs, better housing, better schools, and more opportunities for black Americans to enter the mainstream of U.S. society.

Times indeed had changed.

Chapter Eleven:
The Southwest Georgia Project

The movement continued in southwest Georgia. Two Union students remained for another year doing voter registration, taking time off from seminary as I did. Federal money was gradually working its way into the system, and Head Start and the Community Action Programs were beginning to take hold. Because of the Voting Rights Act of 1965, registering to vote was now less intimidating, and many blacks were registering on their own.

The Southwest Georgia Project for Community Education was officially organized as a separate nonprofit organization in 1968. The organization focused initially on developing youth leaders, promoting African American small businesses, and offering summer enrichment programs and tutoring in rural counties around Albany.

The Southwest Georgia Project's biggest initiative was the New Communities project. Sherrod had come to the conclusion that black ownership of land was essential to the black community's self-determination and independence; in June 1968 he visited Israel as part of a small group from southwest Georgia. Their purpose was to understand Israel's rural land development initiatives and the kibbutz model of communal farming. They came back inspired and decided to develop a large communal farm for African Americans on a land trust to be assembled in southwest Georgia. While farming would be at the core of the effort, the community would address education and governance issues and include other kinds of jobs and initiatives, such as manufacturing. This was occurring at the same time that the concept of new towns was becoming popular in planning circles, and the federal government was starting to provide loan guarantees to permit the development of new towns throughout the country. The official name of the venture was New Communities Inc.

Slater King, a successful real estate professional and brother of the civil rights attorney C. B. King, identified two contiguous farms for sale totaling some fifty-seven hundred acres, in Lee County just north of Albany. New Communities Inc. was able to secure site control and obtain a one-hundred-thousand-dollar planning grant from the Office of Economic Opportunity (OEO). This money was used to bring in outside experts, assess the feasibility of the project, and help forge a vision for the future. The idea was for a utopian community, an American version of a kibbutz. A site plan was created for the entire development, and areas were identified for three different villages, with sites for factories, schools, and other community facilities. It was an ambitious undertaking. At the time, the New Communities land trust was the largest land holding ever under the control of African Americans. The hope was that New Communities would become a model for similar communities across the country.

Charlie's wife, Shirley, a leader in the civil rights movement in her own right, grew up on a farm in Baker County, understood agriculture, and had excellent farming and organizational skills. She and Charlie formed a partnership that provided the energy, leadership, and direction for the effort.

After graduating from Union, Ed Feaver and Joe Pfister returned to work on the project. At first New Communities rented the property, and Sherrod, Feaver, and Pfister spent time raising money. They tried unsuccessfully for a grant from the OEO to allow them to purchase the property. Finally in the mid-1970s they purchased the property with a loan guaranteed by the Farmers Home Administration. While the villages and factories never materialized, the farm produced corn, peanuts, sugar cane, soybeans, and squash on fifteen-hundred of the fifty-seven hundred acres, enough to generate some income. Pfister ran the farm's print shop, which served as a training center for young people. However, ultimately the income from the farm and print shop were not sufficient to pay the debt service and cover the operating expenses. In the mid-1980s the property went into foreclosure.

From the perspective of the twenty-first century, it seems remarkable that New Communities lasted as long as it did—a decade and a half.

While Shirley had farming experience and expertise, few others did; and Charlie ended up recruiting idealistic college-age people, the majority of them white—very much like us volunteers from Union Theological Seminary—to come down and work on the farm, essentially for free. Many lasted only a few days before heading back home. Besides lack of experience in agriculture, New Communities had three other strikes against it. First, farming was changing nationally into fully mechanized agribusiness. New Communities did not have the capital to acquire the machinery necessary for efficient operations. Second, it had acquired a huge land holding with far more land than it could actually put into production, resulting in very high costs to cover the debt. Finally, it had to contend with unfair crop allotments from the Agricultural Stabilization Service, a perennial problem for black farmers.

The unfair experience with crop allotments and the difficulties experienced by black farmers in general influenced Shirley to get involved with the Federation of Southern Cooperatives, where in 1985 she became the director of the Georgia state office and played an instrumental role in getting the U.S. Department of Agriculture to pay black farmers damages for unjust crop allotments. In 2009 Shirley was appointed by President Barack Obama to head the USDA Rural Development office in Georgia. In the spring of 2010 Shirley was the focus of national attention when she was fired by the secretary of agriculture for making allegedly racist comments in a speech to the NAACP, which was shown on a right-wing blog. According to the blog, this video proved that the Obama administration favored blacks and was just as racist as white people were. This got major attention on Fox News and the front pages of the *Washington Post* and *New York Times*.

It took about a day for the truth to come out: the comments that Shirley made were taken out of context and were intended to combat racism, not promote it. In the NAACP speech, what she said was that because of the racism that she experienced and the murder of her father by a white man who was never brought to justice, she was *tempted* to treat poor white farmers differently; but through soul-searching and honest reflection, she concluded that would have been wrong. The case in point was a particular white farmer who was in desperate shape. In the end she helped the white farmer get the resources he needed, and the farmer supported her story. Two days later President Obama called her personally to apologize, and she was offered another job in the Department of Agriculture (which she refused). Shirley became an instant national celebrity.

Charlie turned his attention to local politics. In 1976, while still directing the New Communities project, he was elected to the Albany City Council, on which he served until 1990. In 1996 he ran unsuccessfully for the Georgia state Senate, his last attempt at political office. Following the New Communities effort, he began working in the prison system as a chaplain. He still held this job in 2009 when we attended a southwest Georgia civil rights reunion.

By the end of the 1960s, the days of marches and mass demonstrations were largely over; and while voter registration continued, it was far less controversial. It was paying off big time, however, as black officials like Charlie were being elected at all levels throughout the South. Public schools were being desegregated, albeit slowly, even though Christian—or "rebel yell"—academies were starting to spring up. The movement had certainly made its mark, and life in that part of the world would never go back to the days of Jim Crow.

Chapter Twelve:
1968

Having taken a year off from Union, I prepared at the end of the summer of 1967 to go back to complete my master's of divinity, while Embry would finish up at Barnard. But what would we do after graduating?

The events that had occurred during that summer, along with my experiences in working in secular jobs, pointed me in a new direction. While progress had certainly been made on civil rights, the action had shifted to the cities; and besides it was pretty obvious that the role of whites in the movement was becoming problematic. Rebuilding the cities and providing decent housing became a genuine calling for me, stronger than the calling to become a priest in the Episcopal Church. But I had no skills. I was a history major at Davidson, which did not give me any practical skills, and what good is a degree in theology if you are not going to work in the church?

I immediately went to work thinking about options and within a few weeks had the beginning of a plan. I had long since dismissed going to medical school, law school, or business school. None of these options seemed right for me. Graduate school was also not very appealing since I did not see myself as a college professor. One of my classmates at Union suggested I look into getting a master's in city planning. I hadn't even heard of city planning, but the idea intrigued me. It turned out that Columbia had a department of city planning, so my plan was to take as many city planning courses as I could at Columbia during my last year at Union and try to find fieldwork related to that. When we returned to Union in the fall of 1967, the plan worked out better than I could ever have expected. Not only had I been able to line up a couple of interesting Columbia city planning courses, I was able to get a fieldwork job with the New York City Planning Department. One of my papers for a theology class was on "Making New York Public Housing Projects Human" by providing imaginative playgrounds. And my senior thesis at Union was on the Episcopal Church's role in providing affordable housing and rebuilding inner cities. For the first time at Union, I had classes I really liked, albeit not in theology, and a fieldwork job that I was excited about. I wonder now why they ever allowed me to graduate.

★★★

But everything was not rosy at Union when I returned. In fact, there was a dramatic change in mood and direction—at least among the students. The year before I took the internship, the focus was on civil rights and social justice. In 1967 it was on the war in Vietnam. In the fall of 1965 there was hope and optimism. In the fall of 1967 there was anger and despair.

The popular thing to do in the fall of 1967 and the winter and spring of 1968 was to burn your draft card. Being earnest divinity students and wanting to do the right thing, many of us were ambivalent about getting a deferment for education. In many professional schools and graduate schools, the only reason people were in school in the first place was to get the deferment, but not at Union. There was a collective sense of guilt and an awareness that it was terribly unjust for blue-collar workers to get sent off to the battlefields to fight a senseless war while we graduate students were exempt. By burning our draft cards we would be protesting the war and the injustice of poor people and black people fighting and sacrificing their lives for rich people and white people.

But we could also be going to jail.

When this occurred to me, I began to have second thoughts. What to do? My friends were courageously burning their cards in front of the draft bureau in lower Manhattan and getting arrested. How could I abandon them?

After agonizing over the decision, I announced to Embry that after considerable thought and prayer, I had concluded that my student deferment was wrong, and that I was going to join my friends and burn my draft card.

"Wait a minute," she said. "You don't *have* a student deferment. You have a *physical* deferment because you had polio."

I paused for a long moment.

"Oh yeah, you're right."

I breathed a huge sigh of relief and almost shouted for joy. That was the end of that idea. Another unexpected side benefit of having had polio.

My final year at Union was very different from the first two. I went downtown and supported people who were burning their draft cards, and I did fieldwork off campus for the New York City Planning Department, most of the time in a dilapidated neighborhood in the Bushwick section of Brooklyn, where residents wanted new housing built. In January 1968 Embry, having finished her coursework at Barnard, took a job as a computer programmer for a large company in Midtown. We were living in an off-campus apartment on Riverside Drive about three blocks from Union and loving our new lifestyle.

But there were three things we did not count on. We did not count on the assassination of Martin Luther King Jr. on April 4. We did not count on Columbia, Union, and Barnard all being shut down by student protests during the last two weeks in April. And we did not count on the assassination of Robert Kennedy on June 6. The spring of 1968 was an awful time.

★★★

By 1966, Martin Luther King, like many leaders in the civil rights movement, had taken a different direction. In the spring of 1967, during my year off from Union, King came to New York and preached one of his most famous sermons in Riverside Church, the huge neo-Gothic, nondenominational church next to Union. For the first time he connected the war in Vietnam and the civil rights movement and sharply criticized the United States for being in the war. The sermon, which was delivered on April 4 (a year to the day before his death), was called "Beyond Vietnam." It turned out to be one of King's most controversial speeches, and the mainstream media generally turned against him. *Life* magazine called the speech "demagogic slander that sounded like a script for Radio Hanoi," and the *Washington Post* declared that King had "diminished his usefulness to his cause, his country, his people." He criticized the war on both moral and practical grounds, since it was sapping resources from important domestic initiatives such as the War on Poverty. He pointed to structural issues in the U.S. economy and said, "True compassion is more than flinging a coin to a beggar. . . . It comes to see that an edifice which produces beggars needs restructuring." His subsequent sermons and speeches continued in this vein and became even stronger.

In late 1967 King planned an ambitious new effort to focus on the problems of poverty among all Americans, not just black people. His "Poor People's Campaign" assembled whites and blacks in Washington in the early spring of 1968 to call for an "Economic Bill of Rights"—full employment, a guaranteed annual income for all Americans, and a strong affordable housing program. Except for support from SCLC, King was never able to enlist help from civil rights organizations, most of which had moved toward black nationalism or were focused on local issues. The campaign attracted fewer participants than organizers had hoped for, and press coverage was not extensive. Nothing concrete came of it.

As part of King's new focus on structural economic issues in the American economy, he supported the black sanitary workers' strike in Memphis. Black sanitary workers, who were often paid less than white workers doing the same job, went on strike on March 12, 1968, for better wages and better treatment. They asked King for support, and he traveled there on March 29. On April 3, there was a large rally at Mason Temple, the world headquarters of the Church of God in Christ. There King made his last speech, probably the best known after "I Have a Dream." He seemed to have a premonition of his death. These words have often been quoted:

> And then I got to Memphis. And some began to say the threats, or talk about the threats that were out. What would happen to me from some of our sick white brothers? Well, I don't know what will happen now. We've got some difficult days ahead. But it doesn't matter with me now. Because I've been to the mountain top. And I don't mind. Like anybody, I would like to live a long life. Longevity has its place. But I'm not concerned about that now. I just want to do God's will. And He's allowed me to go up to the mountain. And I've looked over. And I've seen the promised land. I may not get there with you. But I want you to know tonight, that we, as a people, will get to the promised land. And I'm happy, tonight. I'm not worried about

anything. I'm not fearing any man. Mine eyes have seen the glory of the coming of the Lord.

The next day, at 6:01 p.m., King was shot by a single bullet and died one hour later. Violence erupted all over the nation. Disturbances occurred in more than one hundred cities. In Washington a week of clashes destroyed large parts of the city, leaving twelve dead, more than one thousand injured, and more than six thousand arrested.

What I remember about the announcement of King's death was walking into the main student lounge at Union and seeing everyone in the room completely silent, staring at the television. I felt physically ill and like everyone else could only stare.

That day for me marked the end of the civil rights movement.

Two weeks after that Columbia, Barnard, and Union were all shut down as students protested racism and the Vietnam War. The shutdown was sparked by a confrontation between the student radical group, Students for a Democratic Society (SDS), led by Columbia student Mark Rudd, and the police over the construction of a Columbia gymnasium in Morningside Park. There were also accusations that Columbia was secretly supporting the Vietnam War through various research efforts and institutional affiliations.

There were aspects of the Columbia gym that were far from perfect—blacks in Harlem would have to use a separate entrance—but the response seemed to far exceed the malady. Students occupied several buildings on campus, including the president's office, and one of the deans was held hostage. The siege went on for days. Classes were canceled. There were solidarity marches. Union canceled its classes in support of the demonstrators, and Union did not even have a dog in the fight. Finally, when at last I had some classes I actually liked and could understand, they shut the place down. No justice. The siege came to an end in the early morning hours of April 30, when the police moved in with force and arrested some seven hundred protestors, injuring more than 150, several seriously. By that time the semester was almost over and no more classes were held at Union. Everyone got a P for passing.

The final crushing blow was the assassination of Robert Kennedy. Robert Kennedy had a gentle charisma, sincerity, honesty, and self-confidence that made him in my eyes unique among politicians. He was our hope for the future. He was also a friend of Allard Lowenstein, who talked about him in reverential tones when we would gather at Al's West Side apartment with scores of other Al Lowenstein groupies.

We stayed up late the night of the California Democratic primary and watched the returns on television; and when it looked like he had won, we turned off the television and went to bed, pleasantly satisfied. When we turned on the *Today Show* at 7:00 the next morning, we saw the pictures replayed over and over of Kennedy going into the kitchen, surrounded by well-wishers, and then suddenly falling. Embry and I both wept.

★★★

For me, if the King assassination marked the end of the civil rights movement, the Robert Kennedy assassination marked the end of the 1960s—or at least the end of our idealism. Our world would never be the same again. Many of the civil rights leaders had turned to black nationalism. No one could match King's oratory skills or his intellect. We had lost our hope for president and would end up with Richard Nixon.

The period going forward would be very different. The passage of the Fair Housing Act of 1968 sought to address the biggest remaining national racist problem—discrimination against blacks and other minorities in privately owned housing. The bill passed one week after King's assassination.

But the mood of the country had changed. Vietnam War protests became more prevalent and often violent. People seemed to be less hopeful and less optimistic. The new focus was on making the various government programs already on the books work. It was becoming less a time for idealists, reformers, and dreamers and more an opportunity for people with the job skills needed to deal with these problems.

We decided to opt for job skills. In the fall of 1968 we set off for Chapel Hill, where I would get a master's in city and regional planning from the University of North Carolina and study urban development and affordable housing, eventually becoming a housing consultant, specializing in seniors housing and affordable housing. Embry would earn a master's degree in public health, followed some years later by a PhD from George Washington University, and would become an expert in policy research related to maternal and child health.

Our civil rights journey was over.

Postscript

After leaving southwest Georgia in August 1966, Embry and I made three trips back to the area. The first was in the early 1970s, when we stopped to see the Holts on our way to visit my parents in Florida. The Holts and Broadways all gathered at the Holts' house in what felt to me like a family reunion. Jack Holt's eyes had deteriorated, however; although he was only in his late sixties, he was almost blind. This did not keep him from farm work, though he did not live many years after that. Everyone else seemed to be in good shape, the mood was upbeat, and people seemed to be hopeful for the future. Nathan was in high school by then, and Jackie was off to college in Texas.

We did not return until 2007, again on our way to Florida, this time for a family reunion on Embry's side of the family. Baker County seemed to be frozen in time. The population had remained about the same, just under four thousand, and there was not much sign of anything new—except for a new church every so often and a few modest brick homes. Newton for all practical purposes no longer existed. A major flood had wiped out the tiny town more than a decade before, and the only structure preserved was the old courthouse, which was being used in 2007 as a social service agency and museum. It stood eerily alone, with no other buildings in sight. Most government functions had moved to the old school building almost a mile away, the same building where the Head Start program we participated in took place. Also about a mile from the former town was a small, dreary strip shopping center with a gas station, convenience store, and not much else. This was the "new" Newton.

By asking directions at the gas station, we were able to make our way to the sandy road where we had spent that summer, and there we found the Holt house abandoned and dilapidated like all the other houses on that narrow road. We learned from the person at the gas station that Dovanna Holt had died a few years earlier. Her two children were said to be doing well, and at least one was in living in Albany.

After leaving the Holt neighborhood, we visited the old courthouse. On the lower level were several offices and a small museum, and upstairs was the courtroom where we had witnessed the two trials. That room seemed exactly like we remembered it from 1966—white church-like pews facing the judge's bench and the jury section, large ceiling fans, and tall windows allowing the afternoon sun to filter into the room. There were even stacks of old newspapers and what appeared to be legal books stacked in the corner. You expected Sheriff Warren Johnson or C. B. King to walk in at any minute. We remembered exactly where we were sitting when the all-white jury returned after fifteen minutes of deliberation and announced its verdict of guilty for the young black man.

We spent time driving around Baker County. The countryside was as beautiful as ever—vast fields of cotton, peanuts, soybeans, and numerous pecan groves. Pine trees and towering live oaks covered with Spanish moss lined the highway for miles. There were no billboards or anything else to suggest change had happened in Baker County. Except for an occasional passing car or tractor plowing a field, we could have been in the nineteenth century. The only real change we observed was that Ichauway Plantation, owned by the Woodruff family, was now a nonprofit ecological center, open to the public and devoted to education on the environment.

We returned again in June 2009 for the reunion of the Southwest Georgia Project. This time we drove from Atlanta to Albany in a rental car along an interstate that hadn't existed in 1966. We turned off after about two hours and headed toward Albany along a flat stretch of mainly deserted highway, which was four lanes most of the way and seemed to be fairly new. I tried to remember if what we were seeing then was anything like what we had seen when we first entered southwest Georgia forty-three years before. The area did feel different. Though still rural, it was more developed than Baker County. There was an occasional McDonald's or Wendy's and even a Wal-Mart, but not much in the way of new houses or subdivisions.

Albany was hardly recognizable. We arrived on a hot Friday afternoon and checked into a new hotel beside the Flint River. The hotel had a pool, restaurant, and bar. In our room there was a Jacuzzi. Across the street was a riverfront park dedicated to Ray Charles, Albany's most famous native son. Some of the office buildings nearby appeared new, but none were more than a few stories tall. Like so many small towns that have lost virtually all retail to big box stores in the suburbs, downtown Albany on this weekend was deserted, almost a ghost town, even though its population had increased from fifty thousand in 1966 to more than seventy-five thousand in 2009. In 2000 the population was almost two-thirds black. It was probably above 70 percent in 2009. The hotel was only a block or two from where the old SNCC office was located, in a building that in no way resembled my recollection of the place. It actually looked pretty nice. Across the street was the Charles Sherrod Memorial Civil Rights Park and, around the corner, the Albany Civil Rights Museum. Unlike the 1960s, the streets were paved; and the homes, while modest, were in decent shape.

After we settled into the hotel in Albany, we soon ran into several of our friends who worked with us that summer. It was great to see them. Late that afternoon others arrived after a day of touring the counties and towns that were the focus of the movement in 1966—Cordele, Dawson, Colquitt, Baker, Camilla. Sherrod and his wife, Shirley, were there, as were a good number of local movement people. Since everyone was by now in "advanced middle age," people might have mistaken us for a senior citizens convention. Some of the national SNCC workers from those times attended, though no one I remembered. The mood was ebullient, and there were the usual hugs and embraces. In all there were about twenty or twenty-five white people, and at least an equal number of blacks along with some of their children and grandchildren, mainly from the Albany area. The SNCC Freedom Singers originated in Albany; and one of the founders, Rutha Harris, still lived there. Soon she was leading us in some of the movement songs—"Oh, Freedom," "We Shall Overcome," "Will the Circle Be Unbroken?" and many others, some long forgotten. The singing was terrific. Had it been necessary back then to audition before joining SNCC?

The reunion continued all day on Saturday at Albany State University, the historically African American school located across the Flint River from our hotel, and concluded on Sunday. Plans were discussed for an even bigger reunion in a couple of years to mark the fiftieth anniversary of the civil rights movement in Albany. There were stories and more stories. I had forgotten that members of our group had been shot at, roughed up by police, and threatened; and I had forgotten how prevalent fear was for many of the movement people. I was thankful that we had been tucked away in Baker County, out of sight of most of the really hostile white folks, or "crackers" as the SNCC workers called them.

One of the most interesting events was when we went around the room and talked about what the movement meant to us and what we were doing now. Many testimonies were eloquent. Some said that the movement was the most important event in their life, that it had changed them forever.

As far as I could tell, my fellow seminarians from Union for the most part had had good jobs and satisfying careers. Sherrod, after fourteen years on the Albany City Council, was now chaplain at the state prison. Shirley had a big job with the U.S. Department of Agriculture. Feaver had been secretary of the Florida Department of Children and Families in the 1990s. Ashley ran the legal aid program in Middle Tennessee. One person was a religion professor at Vassar College and probably the world's foremost expert on the black church, one an acupuncturist living near Chapel Hill, one a former minister from California (about the only person I can recall at Union who went this route) and now an elementary school teacher there, and another a child psychiatrist near Cleveland. These were my closest friends. Others had similar careers. Not bad, I thought, for a bunch of unstable Union Seminary students, who for the most part in 1966 had no clue what they wanted to do with their lives.

Embry was one of the last to speak, just before me. She talked about how important the experience was for us. She brought people up to date on our story—her career in health policy research and mine in affordable housing and seniors housing, still living in Washington, with two children and four grandchildren in New Jersey and New Hampshire. She thanked everyone for making the reunion happen and for the opportunity to work in the movement in 1966. She echoed the feelings expressed by so many—that it had been a once in a lifetime opportunity.

During the storytelling and personal testimonies there had been some talk about how young people today had no idea how hard the civil rights struggle was and how important it was for them to know the truth and to hear the stories of those who had worked on the frontlines. When Embry sat down and my turn came to speak, I said I agreed that there was nothing more important than keeping the flame alive and educating our young people as to what really happened on the frontlines of the civil rights movement in the 1960s. This comment prompted several comments of "Amen, brother."

"In fact," I continued, "I dedicated my life to this effort, starting with my own two children. I knew I had succeeded when my son proudly showed me a paper he had written for his eighth-grade social studies class in Washington, D.C., which started off, 'There were three great leaders of the Civil Rights Movement, Martin Luther King Junior, John Lewis, and *my dad*, Joseph T. Howell.'"

This brought the house down.

The highlight of the weekend was getting back in touch with the Holt boys, now the Holt men. Jackie had been seventeen and Nathaniel twelve in 1966; and while they seemed then to be in a different generation from us, Jackie was only three years younger than Embry and six years younger than me. Two years earlier Embry had tried to get in touch with Jackie and Nathaniel before we ventured south to Baker County on the way to the family reunion in Florida. The Internet helped her locate Nathaniel, who was living in Albany. We were not able to see him on that trip but promised to try to do so in the future. He said that Jackie was living in San Francisco and the reason we could not find him on the Internet was that he now went by his given name, Noah.

By the 2009 reunion, Jackie had returned with his wife to Albany; and he called us before the reunion to make sure we got together. Midway through the Saturday afternoon session we left the reunion activities; and with Ashley and his wife, Susan, and Meredy, our friend from Cleveland, we headed out to the suburbs to visit Jackie. We traveled several miles through one middle-class subdivision after another before arriving at a very attractive ranch-style house with a large yard situated beside a pond. A middle-aged man—Jackie was by then fifty-seven—greeted us with a broad grin and a big hug and introduced us to his wife of thirty-plus years.

Jackie and his wife proudly showed us around their house. They had several photos of Muhammad Ali on the wall along with pictures of Martin Luther King Jr. and pictures of Jackie's father and mother, Jack and Dovanna. Their home was tastefully and unpretentiously decorated and had a warm feel to it. We sat out on the screened-in back porch, drank cold lemonade, and spent the rest of the afternoon talking. Midway through the conversations Nathan appeared. Five years younger, he seemed more recognizable than his brother, still having his boyish face. Both men looked very good and appeared to be in good health.

Jackie left Newton in 1967, the summer after we were there, to attend a small, historically black college in Texas, where he met his wife. They married after college and moved to Palo Alto, California, where both attended Stanford University graduate school. His wife received a master's in business administration there. They settled in the San Francisco Bay Area, where they both ended up in top management positions, Jackie working for a railroad company and his wife in financial management for a major health insurance firm. They had one married daughter and one grandchild. In different years they each had received the Martin Luther King Distinguished Community Service Award in the Bay Area, the first time two people from the same family had received this prestigious honor.

They moved back to Albany in order to find a more low-key lifestyle. After returning to Albany, Jackie took a job as "international site selection chairman" for his college fraternity. The job required some travel, but he worked out of his house, and the job was part-time and less stressful.

Nathaniel attended Albany State but did not finish; but he had held solid government jobs and seemed happy. He was still shy and had the same smile and twinkle in his eye. Next time he promised to bring his wife along. Jackie and Nathan both still attended their old church in Baker County every Sunday, a drive of about thirty-five miles in each direction.

I thought how proud Mrs. Holt would be of her children. Could these life stories have happened before the civil rights movement? While there was still much to be done and steps backward for every step forward, I could not help smiling and thinking what a long way we had come since 1966.

Jackie had lots of stories. One that got my attention was a face-off between the Holt family and the Ku Klux Klan, which occurred the year before we arrived and happened in the front yard of the Holt house. Guns were drawn on both sides, but no fire was exchanged when the Klan realized the Holts were not bluffing. Another was an incident during demonstrations at the courthouse in 1965 when his father almost got into a fight with an angry white mob. A third involved leasing the Holt farm after his mother died to a white farmer who had been—and probably still was—one of the worst racists in the county. All I could think of was how glad I was I had not heard the first two stories that summer of 1966. When asked why no one had told us about these incidents, Jackie said they did not want us to be afraid.

During the course of the conversation, Jackie left the back porch and returned with a large black and white photo I had taken of his family and the Broadways in 1971, when we were traveling through the area on our way to visit my parents in Florida. He said he had made copies for all the people in the photograph and that the photo could be found on the walls of everyone he had given it to.

He also turned to me toward the end of the day and said, "Joe, you know you changed my life." By "you" I'm sure he meant all of us, but for some reason he turned and looked me straight in the eye. "If it had not been for you, for what you did that summer, for you being with my family and for showing us that all white people weren't evil, for showing us what *we* could be, there is no way that I would have done what I've done or be who I am."

I was dumbfounded. On our way to the car, Ashley's wife, Susan, pulled me over and said, "Joe, that was some tribute." It was a tribute not only to me but to all of us. I suppose you could say it vindicated and affirmed the entire experience. We ventured down to southwest Georgia in hopes of doing our small part to make a difference. But so often you do not know what impact you are having. I certainly never dreamed that we had had such an influence on Jackie.

★★★

I look back on the summer of 1966 with the kind of nostalgia that often accompanies such experiences. I imagine that in some ways our experience was not that different from that of a Peace Corps volunteer. Were it not for the diary maybe I would have forgotten the darker moments and times of confusion and uncertainty. Finding that dusty, long-forgotten document brought back the complete experience.

In reading the diary again and wrapping it in memoir and history, I am taken by the times we lived in. Has there ever been a period in America when so much social change happened so fast? Has there ever been a better time to be young and idealistic? My children, who are now in their thirties and forties, understood this even when they were much younger. I remember my son saying when he was in college, "Dad, you were so lucky to grow up at a time in American history when the issues were so obvious. Back then it was pretty easy to get it right. Nowadays there seems to be a lot more uncertainty as to how to tackle our problems."

I agreed but reminded him that at the time a lot of people did not see it that way and that it was also a painful time. We lost John Kennedy, Martin Luther King, and Robert Kennedy. Many others died or were seriously wounded in the civil rights struggle.

But my son was basically right. The issues—especially in the mid-1960s—were obvious. Segregation was wrong and had to end. To be part of the civil rights movement was an extraordinary privilege. We felt connected, part of history. We *were* so lucky.

Suggested Reading

Bass, S. Jonathan. *Blessed Are the Peacemakers: Martin Luther King Jr., Eight White Religious Leaders, and the "Letter from Birmingham Jail."* Baton Rouge: Louisiana State University Press, 2001.

Branch, Taylor. *Parting the Waters: America in the King Years, 1954–63.* New York: Simon and Schuster, 1988.

———. *Pillar of Fire: America in the King Years, 1963–65.* New York: Simon and Schuster, 1998.

———. *Canaan's Edge: America in the King Years, 1965–68.* New York: Simon and Schuster, 2006.

Halberstam, David. *The Children.* New York: Fawcett, 1998.

Hampton, Henry, and Steve Fayer, with Sarah Flynn. *Voices of Freedom: An Oral History of the Civil Rights Movement from the 1950s through the 1980s.* New York: Bantam, 1990.

Hogan, Wesley C. *Many Minds, One Heart: SNCC's Dream for a New America.* Chapel Hill: University of North Carolina Press, 2007.

Kluger, Richard. *Simple Justice: The History of Brown v. Board of Education and Black America's Struggle for Equality.* Rev. ed. New York: Vintage, 2004.

Lewis, John, with Michael D'Orso. *Walking with the Wind: A Memoir of the Movement.* New York: Harvest, 1998.

McAdam, Doug. *Freedom Summer.* New York: Oxford University Press, 1988.

Myers, C. Kilmer. *Light the Dark Streets.* Greenwich, Conn.: Seabury, 1957.

Warren, Mark R. *Fire in the Heart: How White Activists Embrace Racial Justice.* New York: Oxford University Press, 2010.

Watson, Bruce. *Freedom Summer: The Savage Season That Made Mississippi Burn and America a Democracy.* New York: Viking, 2010.

Winter, Gibson. *The Suburban Captivity of the Churches: An Analysis of Protestant Responsibility in the Expanding Metropolis.* New York: Macmillan, 1962.